THRYMSAS AND SCEATTAS
IN THE ASHMOLEAN MUSEUM OXFORD

THRYMSAS AND SCEATTAS

IN THE ASHMOLEAN MUSEUM OXFORD

VOLUME 2

BY

D. M. METCALF

Keeper of the Heberden Coin Room

ROYAL NUMISMATIC SOCIETY AND
ASHMOLEAN MUSEUM OXFORD
LONDON
1993

Royal Numismatic Society
Special Publication No.27B
ISBN   1   85444   066   7

British Library Cataloguing in Publication Data

Metcalf, D. M.
  Thrymsas and Sceattas
  in the Ashmolean Museum
  I. Title
  737.4

Typeset by Lasercomp at
Oxford University Computing Service
Printed in Great Britain
by the Cambridge University Press

CONTENTS

PART III

Continental sceattas 169
Distinguishing the places of origin of
   Series D and E 174
The continental runic sceattas of Series D,
    Type 2c 184
Series D, Type 8 191
Series E: the four early varieties of porcupines 196
Series E: the later porcupines 222
Series E, Type 53 (porcupine/stepped cross) 243
Two rare porcupine 'mules' 246
BMC Type 10 248
'Madelinus' denarii (Series Ma) 251
Where were the so-called 'Herstal' and
   'Maastricht' types minted? 255
The western limits of the spread of sceattas
   in Normandy 263
Series G 266
Danish sceattas: Series X 275

vii

CONTINENTAL SCEATTAS

WHETHER from a numismatic or a monetary point of view, there is little difference between a Merovingian silver denarius and a sceat. The flans are much the same size, and the weights and alloy contents are within the same range. Early antiquaries in England, with very little detailed evidence on which to base their attributions, gave currency to the term 'sceattas' for the late-seventh and eighth-century pre-penny coinages found in southern England. Similarly, numismatists of the early nineteenth century on the Continent referred to Merovingian denarii as 'saigas', a term found in the Bavarian and German law codes. It is nowadays completely obsolete. Many of the sceattas found in England were, as we now know, minted on the Continent, but strict proof of that was not forthcoming, for some of the types in question, until quite recently. The instinctive judgement of the antiquaries was sound, in recognizing the affinity of the English and continental sceattas. One can see at a glance the difference in general style between the characteristic Merovingian denarii with moneyers' names, and characteristic sceattas, but there is no clear boundary between them, and it is difficult to construct a logical definition. Most (but not all) sceattas are anepigraphic or have meaningless legends; but so are some Merovingian coins. The simplest solution would be to abolish the use of the word 'sceattas' altogether, and to follow Stewart, in speaking about 'the early English denarial coinage.'[1] Before one can do that, however, one has to decide whether the particular sceatta types in question are English or Merovingian – or Frisian, or Danish. An all-purpose name does not dispose of the need to resolve the question 'where', which has to be addressed as a separate exercise for each type.

Even if one can be confident that a type is Frisian, some ambiguity

[1] I. Stewart, 'The early English denarial coinage, c.680-c.750' in *Sceattas in England and on the Continent*, edited by D. Hill and D. M. Metcalf, Oxford, 1984, pp.5-26.

remains, in that people who spoke Old Frisian, and thought of themselves as Frisian, lived on both sides of the political frontier of the Merovingian realm, along the lower Rhine. Sceatta types may well have been imitated across the frontier, and it is optimistic to suppose that we can be sure, even now, of the political authority under which all continental sceattas were minted.

In the late seventh century there was a common market in the North Sea coastlands, and English monetary influences spilled over onto the Continent. Series C of the sceattas was imitated by the 'continental runic' type, minted somewhere in the area of the Rhine distributaries. The square banner or standard of Series A and C was similarly copied as the reverse of the porcupine type, which became the most prolific of all sceattas. The great scale of its issue reflects the commercial dominance of Dorestad, where the trade of the Rhinelands met the sea-routes which ran eastwards along the Frisian coast, and in the other direction to northern France, and southern and eastern England. Much of the North Sea trade was in the hands of Frisian merchants and seamen. Their enterprise resulted in the mingling of currencies from as far apart as Northumbria and Jutland. The commerce out of Dorestad and other ports of the Rhine mouths resulted in a net inflow of coinage into England in the late seventh and early eighth centuries.

The sceatta coinages thus extend onto the Continent, to include four major series, and several minor ones. The big four, which Rigold included in his scheme of classification, are Series D, E, G, and X. The minor coinages include *BMC* Type 10, which is a D/E 'mule', and possibly two or three other scarce types which have been found on both sides of the Channel. Even the large coinages have proved difficult to attribute correctly to their region of origin. Because specimens are frequently found in England as well as on the Continent, their classification was regarded as uncertain by earlier generations of numismatists. Rigold treated Series F as continental too, as its place in his alphabetical scheme indicates. He regarded Series D, E, F, and G as 'intermediate'. The question of their overlap in date with the English primary and secondary phases has already been discussed.

The basic argument for attribution is that we should expect a coinage to be most plentiful in its region of origin. Thus, the ubiquitous porcupines (Series E) make up almost 50 per cent of the finds from the area of the Rhine mouths, but only 20 per cent of the finds from England. Although the evidence needs to be scrutinized, and supported by a variety of supplementary arguments, the contrast between 50 per cent

170

and 20 per cent is the basic reason for asserting that porcupines are, in general, continental.

There can be practical difficulties in working out the same sort of argument for other series, if it so happens that little information about single finds is available from the place of origin, or if the type is a scarce one, for which the finds are too few to permit statistically secure conclusions. The **VERNVS** and **SAROALDO** types and Series W are all examples of coinages where it proved difficult until recently to decide whether they were continental or English. They have been discussed above as English primary types.

Domburg, with its magnificent series of almost a thousand site-finds of sceattas, is by far the best point of reference. Types which were so scarce that they might be expected to make up only 1 per cent of the assemblage, or even 0.5 per cent, can be detected there, whereas their absence from a site from which we have a mere hundred finds may be a matter of chance, without significance. From Dorestad, for all its commercial importance, we have fewer than a hundred site-finds of sceattas and contemporary coins, – barely enough to establish the proportions of the half-dozen most plentiful types securely. Even so, these are archaeological riches compared with evidence from the coastlands of Belgium and northern France. There, the merest handful of eighth-century single finds is on record, and it seems that that is genuine negative evidence, rather than merely an absence of evidence. Since 1981 the *Revue du Nord* has maintained a 'Chronique numismatique' recording local finds. Almost all the finds are of Roman coins, one exception being a 'plumed bird' porcupine from Le Portel (Pas-de-Calais).[2] It may be that the only major concentration of sceattas on the coasts west of Domburg was at Quentovic. The attribution of a substantial series of sceattas to Quentovic, however, will remain very speculative unless new archaeological discoveries are made there. Series G may have been minted there, but the best arguments that can be offered at present depend on excluding its attribution elsewhere. In Jutland, information was as sparse as it is in Picardy and Normandy, until 1973, when excavations at Ribe began to yield astonishing quantities of Series X, which we can now see to be Danish.

Three distinctive coin-types are marginal to the sceatta series. The

[2] R. Delmaire, D. Gricourt, P. Leclercq, *et al.*, 'Chronique numismatique' (IX), *Revue du Nord* 72 (1990), no.286, 179-85, where earlier instalments are listed. The Le Portel find is illustrated in *Revue du Nord* 70 (1988) no.276, at p.195. The relatively few sceatta finds from Belgium (but not northern France) up to 1984 are gathered up in W. Op den Velde, W. J. de Boone, and A. Pol, 'A survey of sceatta finds from the Low Countries', in *Sceattas in England and on the Continent*, at pp.143-4.

Madelinus denarii, continuing an issue of gold originally minted at Dorestad, are Merovingian in their general appearance, but may be an immobilized type minted elsewhere; perhaps beyond the frontier, in Frisian territory. For that reason they can usefully be considered along with the sceattas. The so-called 'Herstal' and 'Maastricht' types are anepigraphic coinages which were hoarded alongside sceattas in Frisia, and which occur as stray losses at Dorestad and Domburg. Unlike Series D and E they were very rarely carried to England. Their mint-places are uncertain. They have been included here for the sake of completeness.

I

Hoards play a greater part in our understanding of the continental issues of sceattas than they do in England, where West Hougham, Aston Rowant, and Middle Harling are the only large finds. From Frisian territory, there are large hoards from Remmerden, Hallum, Terwispel, Lutje Saaksum, an unknown locality in Friesland, Kloster Barthe, Föhr, and Franeker. They play a greater part in the analysis because the number of sites from which single finds have been published is far fewer than in England. Also, there is less interaction with the political geography of the regions where sceattas are found than in England, which was a patchwork of small kingdoms issuing their own coinages. The continental hoards are mostly *Auslandsfunde*, akin to the later Viking-age treasures of the Northern Lands in that respect. Their value arises out of their age-structure and out of what they demonstrate about the internal chronology of Series D, E, and X and – even more precious evidence – about the relative chronology of these and various English series of sceattas. Most of the hoards are virtually one-type hoards, but Hallum is of mixed composition and special importance.

Something similar is true of the French hoards of Saint-Pierre-les-Etieux, Plassac, Nohanent, Bais, and Cimiez, in which sceattas form only a small proportion of the contents. They should be used circumspectly, because there can be no certainty that a few strays, concealed far away from their region of origin, were of the same date as the more recent coins in such hoards.

II

The chronology of the continental sceattas is clearer at its beginning than at its end. From the range of varieties present in the Remmerden and

Aston Rowant hoards, one can argue that Series D and E began *c.*695. The Hallum hoard, in which the whole range of varieties of Series X was already represented, suggests an origin for that series in *c.*710. Series G is more difficult to date, but it too is already present in the Garton-on-the-Wolds grave-find and in the Hallum hoard, pointing again to an origin in *c.*710-15. The issue of sceattas was brought to an end in the Rhine mouths area by the arrival of the denarii of Pepin's reform. The Franeker varieties of porcupine are evidently among the latest, but whether they were still in issue at the date of the reform is uncertain. In Jutland the circulation of Series X is very well dated by stratigraphy and dendrochronology from Ribe, from the 1990 excavations of the Post Office site. The archaeological evidence shows that the Wodan-monster sceattas first appear, in quantities, early in layer C, which is dated to *c.*720-740/50. The numbers of finds of sceattas dwindle progressively through layers D, E, and F. The finds cease in layer G, which begins *c.*770/80. The broad-flan 'Hedeby' coins, which are far less plentiful, turn up in layer I.

For Series G there is no corresponding wealth of information. The type appears to begin in the 710s or thereabouts, and to be relatively short-lived.

DISTINGUISHING THE PLACES OF ORIGIN
OF SERIES D AND E

THE 'continental runic' and 'porcupine' sceattas, Series D and E respectively, exist today in great quantities, having come to light in large hoards and also very plentifully as single finds. Series D comprises two easily recognizable types, *BMC* Types 2c and 8, which share a distinctive reverse design. Series E was listed in *BMC* as Types 5 and 6, but that division does not do justice to the profusion of varieties that occur. There seems to be no end to the different dies that are found: both series, but particularly the porcupines, were originally minted in vast quantities. In the random sample of finds from England in the 1980s (Table 1 above) D and E account for 6.4 and 20.7 per cent of all the finds respectively. Porcupines far outnumber any other series in England, their nearest rivals being R, with 7.8 and Y with 7.7 per cent. But in the Low Countries they are even more dominant. At Domburg, and also at Wijk-bij-Duurstede (Dorestad) Series E makes up 47 per cent of all sceatta finds.[1] Series D is also much more plentiful at Domburg than in England, accounting for 21 per cent of the finds. At Dorestad, a more modest 7 per cent of the sceattas are of Series D. In the Rhine valley porcupines are the common sceatta type. Elsewhere on the Continent – in northern France, and even in Jutland – the two series are roughly as plentiful, compared with other types, as they are in England.

Where were they minted? One might expect them to be most plentiful in their region of origin, and less so as they were carried further afield and came into competition, in the make-up of the statistics, with the local issues of other regions. The absolute numbers of finds from one region as compared with another will be influenced by chance, but percentages based on all the finds from one region as against another should discount that variation, and allow us to make even-handed comparisons.[2] If the

---

[1] W. Op den Velde, W. J. de Boone, and A. Pol, 'A survey of sceatta finds from the Low Countries', in *Sceattas in England and on the Continent*, edited by D. Hill and D. M. Metcalf, Oxford, 1984, pp.117-145.

[2] D. M. Metcalf, 'A note on sceattas as a measure of international trade, and on the earliest Danish coinage', ibid., pp.159-64.

theory of diffusion is accepted, it will follow that Series D and E are in general continental, not English, sceattas (in spite of their being among the most plentiful types found in England) and their mints of origin will be sought probably in the area of the Rhine mouths. On the evidence set out so far, it is theoretically possible that they belong somewhere else, in a region where they were even more plentiful than at Domburg and Dorestad, but from which by chance we have few or no finds. We are speaking, however, about a prolific mint or mints, of which the size alone should limit the choice of location. If the porcupines all belong to the same place, it will have been easily the largest mint of the North Sea coastlands in the early eighth century, more active than London or the east Kentish mint or the Ipswich mint. Archaeological exploration of some 30 hectares of the northern part of Dorestad has revealed the great extent of the port there, with wharves stretching for at least two kilometres. Although the total number of sceattas recovered at Dorestad is only about 60, that figure reflects merely the chances of archaeological excavation and the reporting of casual finds, and it is not in any sense a useful index of the volume of monetary transactions in the wic, as compared with Domburg, for example, from where a thousand finds are recorded. Given the archaeological context of a major wic, and given the 47 per cent representation of porcupines among the finds there, it is natural to suppose that they are, essentially, the distinctive coin type minted at Dorestad. There is no sense in postulating an archaeologically unknown or unrecognized mint-place of even greater commercial importance, where porcupines would, if we knew about them, make up even more than 47 per cent of the finds.

The general theory of diffusion may need to be modified, however, in its application to the porcupines, which enjoyed such a widespread vogue that they may well have been subject to imitation. Their mint-place lay on or near a political frontier, beyond which Merovingian rulers could exercise little or no control over the coinage. Dorestad's importance as a mint arose precisely out of its frontier role in trade with more northerly lands. In Frisia, enterprising mint-masters may have struck porcupines with impunity, for their customers to take to England or Jutland and trade with there. They may, moreover, have compromised the reputation of the porcupines for reliability of alloy, by making imitations of a somewhat inferior quality. Such activity may help to explain the endless stylistic diversity of the porcupines. Mints are not to be multiplied unnecessarily, and we should accept the hypothesis of secondary mint-places for the porcupines only in so far as we are driven to it. We can see, meanwhile, that in the particular historical context of the porcupines, there may have been places of modest importance beyond the frontier where the percentage of porcupines exceeded 47, but that they will not affect our judgement that Dorestad was the real home of the type. Opportunist copying may modify the normal patterns of the geographical diffusion of coin types, and our stylistic analysis of a complex issue should bear that possibility in mind.

It will not affect our conviction that the mint of a large wic normally kept to its own distinctive design of sceattas, often for decades on end, for obvious reasons of commercial advantage and confidence, in a barely literate society. We should therefore be disposed to look for a second mint-place, other than Dorestad, for Series D, which was struck concurrently with the early part of E. What of Domburg itself, with its thousand finds? Does not that enormous total effectively prove that Domburg was a busy wic, which would have had its own coinage? It might seem to be a counter-argument that Domburg is apparently not referred to in any contemporary sources as an important trading place; but neither is Ipswich mentioned until the tenth century. The silence of the sources should not be taken as negative evidence. Domburg has exactly the same percentage of porcupines as Dorestad (47 per cent), which at first sight is curious. It has, however, many more coins of Series D (21 per cent, against 7 per cent at Dorestad). D is far more plentiful at Domburg than at any other site known to us. We should concentrate on the ratio of D to E, namely one to 2.2 at Domburg, but one to 6.7 at Dorestad. The figures are understandable if there was diffusion in both directions, but if Dorestad was much the larger mint. As Series E heavily outnumbers D further afield, for example in England and in Denmark, that seems a reasonable assumption.

The alternative, namely that both Series D and E were minted at Dorestad, perhaps at different dates – in the same way that Series A and K were both minted in east Kent, for example, at different dates, can be dismissed on the evidence of the English grave-finds. These can be arranged into a compact chronological sequence on the basis of the varieties of Series A and B they contain. Series C appears for the first time in the Southend-on-Sea find, and C and D together in Birchington.[3] A recent group of 20 coins from the Kings Lynn area, conjecturally a grave-find, is a little later again, containing A (1), B (3), C (5), D (3), E (4), BZ (1), Z (1), F (1) and the earliest variety of R (1).[4] The numbers of

---

[3] S. E. Rigold, 'The two primary series of sceattas', *BNJ* 30 (1960-1), 6-53. The grave-finds terminating with C are Southend-on-Sea, and with C and D, Birchington.

[4] *Dans le commerce.* The coins were purchased as a lot of 21 by a dealer, the odd coin being clearly intrusive. The patina was uniform, and the rarities help to authenticate the find.

specimens of D are far too small to be statistically reliable, but the Birchington and Kings Lynn finds demonstrate that D originated very soon after the introduction of C (which it imitates), and they suggest that E originated a year or two later, if not at the same time: one of the four porcupines is a coin that would automatically be labelled secondary.

The chronology is tight: in Aston Rowant we already see a very wide range, possibly the complete stylistic range, of Series D.[5] To allow space for its development, the origin of D needs to be pushed back as far as possible from the date of concealment of Aston Rowant (c.705-10). And the porcupines in Aston Rowant already include, for example, Varieties G1 (2), G2 (2), G3 (3),[6] and G 4.[7] Their origin, too, must be pushed back several years earlier than c.710.

It is clear enough, then, that there is a substantial overlap between D and the earlier ('intermediate') varieties of E. It offends against one's numismatic instincts to think that two such different designs could have been issued simultaneously in one place. Moreover, had that happened – and the one place would then have to be Dorestad – there is no obvious reason why relatively so many more coins of Series D than E should have been carried from there to Domburg (but see below).

As Domburg is not known from the written sources, we should consider whether the mint-place of Series D could lie further to the west – perhaps even as far west as Quentovic, which is often mentioned as a port. The reason for looking westwards is that the ratio of Series D to E is more in favour of D in the French hoards. At Dorestad, as we have seen, the ratio is about 1 to 7, and at Domburg 2 to 5, whereas in the Bais hoard (from Brittany) the proportions are reversed: 17 coins to 8, or 2 to 1. In the Saint-Pierre-les-Etieux hoard it was 3 to 5, and at Nohanent 1 to 1. From the sand dunes at De Panne, at the western end of the Belgian coast, it was 3 to 2.[8] Although the numbers on which these ratios are based are small, they point consistently to a sphere where the influence of Series D was as great as that of E or greater. We lack a sufficient number of finds from Quentovic to know whether or not that place minted its own distinctive type of sceattas. The same argument from diffusion and the same hypothesis of adherence to one particular design may one day be possible. The prediction is ventured below that archaeological exploration will eventually confirm that Series G belongs to Quentovic. That

[5] An assessment based on published and unpublished photographs of various parcels coming from the Aston Rowant hoard.

[6] M. A. S. Blackburn and M. J. Bonser, 'The "porcupine" sceattas of Metcalf's Variety G', BNJ 57 (1987), 99-103.

[7] Glendining 17 February 1988, lot 283c (not illustrated), doubtless from Aston Rowant.

[8] Metcalf, loc.cit. (note 2 above).

leaves no room there for Series D, in spite of its westerly occurrence on the Continent.

In any case, Series D in England has a well-defined East Anglian and east-coast distribution consistent with its arrival on the back of the North Sea trade. If it had been minted at Quentovic, one would have expected to see more of it at Hamwic, and in Kent, Sussex, and Wessex generally. Its English distribution, in short, would have looked more like that of Series G.

The evidence of the site-finds, then, is that the porcupine type belongs, with very little doubt, to Dorestad, and the continental runic type to another, smaller mint with a somewhat more westerly sphere of influence, but still within the orbit of the North Sea trade which reached along England's eastern coasts. It is very possibly from Domburg, the site of which has been so prolific in sceatta finds as to create an argument for the existence of a mint there.

One can continue to add supporting detail, for example by attempting an analysis of the finds from the region nearest to Dorestad. At Maurik and Rijswijk, on the River Lek just a few kilometres upstream from Dorestad, a combined total of 28 coins have been dredged out of the river. The proportion of Series D to E among them matches that among the 60 specimens from Dorestad, adding usefully to the rather thin and at times vague numismatic record from the site itself.[9]

Extra detail, however, does little to buttress the argument at the point where it is logically weakest. It has been assumed for the purpose of the numerical comparisons not only that the site-finds are random losses in respect of their types, i.e. that a coin stood an equal chance of being accidentally lost whether it was of Series D or E, but also that Series D remained in use, and therefore available to be accidentally lost, over much the same span of years at Domburg as at Dorestad, and similarly with Series E. There is no positive reason to question that assumption, but stating it helps to show the importance of the hoard evidence, from which the relative chronology of the two series can be assessed. A general decline in the rate of coin losses at Domburg in the later stages of the intermediate phase, for whatever reason – climatic or environmental changes, or greater exposure to the Viking threat – could well have been enough to distort the ratios of D and E, which if taken globally will necessarily reflect an average of the relative loss-rates throughout the period of currency. Thus if Series E gradually gained numerical superiority, that in itself might partly account for the statistical difference

---

[9] W. Op den Velde, 'Sceatta's gevonden bij Maurik en Rijswijk', *JMP* 69 (1962), 5-19.

between Domburg and Dorestad. The finds of Carolingian coins at the two sites show that the longer-term trend was one of increasing numbers of losses at Dorestad into the later eighth and ninth centuries, and decreasing numbers at Domburg.[10]

If the sites had different histories, that should impose a degree of caution on our interpretation of the statistical differences. Still, the tendency of the argument would be to reinstate the possibility that Series D and E could both belong to Dorestad. We may feel entitled to discount it because 'one wic – one type' is so often the rule elsewhere.

We return to the position that E belongs to Dorestad, and D very probably to Domburg. Against that, however, the evidence of the Remmerden hoard is problematic. The sceattas are almost all of Series D, with only a few strays of Series E and other types.[11] But the find-spot is much closer to Dorestad than to Domburg – in fact, only a few kilometres upstream from Maurik. Unless D were earlier than E, we have a sum of money in which the proportion of D to E – 136 specimens against 7 – far exceeds the figures of one to 2.2 among the Domburg site-finds, let alone one to 6.7 at Dorestad. The Remmerden sceattas are essentially a one-type hoard, either because they were withdrawn from the currency of a place where Series D was in almost exclusive use, or because the owner deliberately selected sceattas of Series D. If Series E had just been introduced when the Remmerden hoard was concealed, we would expect to find only the very earliest issues of E included in it. The seven porcupines are indeed of Aston Rowant varieties, but again, two of them are of Variety G4 (reading AZO), which certainly belongs late in the sequence represented at Aston Rowant.

Is there any possibility of a flaw in the argument, meaning that Series D in fact belongs to Dorestad, or are we compelled to say that Remmerden is a traveller's hoard, assembled in a different place from that in which it was concealed? We should have no hesitation in preferring the evidence of the site-finds, which reflect the balance of hundreds of separate incidents when one coin was randomly lost, over the single incident of the concealment of a hoard, put together in circumstances which in principle we cannot possibly reconstruct from its composition.

The Aston Rowant hoard also raises problems of interpretation when it is set alongside the site finds. It, too, reverses the normal ratios of D to E. We shall probably never know the hoard's exact composition, but the large section of it published in *Coin Hoards* contained 162 specimens of

[10] H. H. Völckers, *Karolingische Münzfunde der Frühzeit (751-800)*, Göttingen, 1965, s.v.

[11] I am indebted to Mr. A. Pol for advance information about the hoard.

Type 2c (plus 17 of Type 8) against about 60 porcupines.[12] Similar comments apply. So large a proportion of coins of Series D cannot have been gathered out of the English currency, unless by persistent selection. It will be natural to think of them as a sum of money carried more or less *en bloc* to England.

Another potential logical weakness in our interpretation of the site-finds, already touched on, is that the argument has so far been conducted on the basis that Series D (Type 2c) and E are each from a single mint-place. Each has been treated as a unit. But we need to consider the numerical implications if a type as prevalent and successful as the porcupines was imitated at another mint-place, or at more than one other mint-place. The same consideration applies to Series D. Statistics which treat the two series each as a whole will conceal the geographical origin of any such imitative varieties.

The early, 'Aston Rowant' phase of Series E comprises four substantive varieties, each quite different as regards both obverse and reverse designs: the 'plumed bird' design; the 'VICO' variety; Metcalf Variety G, with an insect-like design; and Metcalf Variety D.[13] Each of these is so different that it is puzzling to imagine that they were all minted in Dorestad. Of course, we need not suppose that in the early eighth century there was 'a mint' there, in the sense either of a building to which a number of moneyers went each day to work, or an organization to which moneyers belonged. Several men may have worked independently, from their own premises. Even so, the designs seem to have less in common than one would have expected. The question whether they could have been minted at more than one town on the lower Rhine – or whether any of the varieties could be English copies, or for that matter copies made at Domburg – has not been addressed merely by demonstrating from the over-all statistics that the majority of porcupines are continental. The same comparative arguments would need to be repeated in miniature, separately for each variety. For places close together on the distributaries of the Rhine, the geographical problem seems almost insoluble. For England it should not be too difficult, given accurate information to analyse, because an issue that was minted in England might be expected to generate a different distribution pattern from an issue that was imported. If one (or more) of the varieties were

[12] J. P. C. Kent, in *Oxoniensia* 37 (1972), 243-4; *CH* 1 (1975), 87; Glendinings 13 March 1975, lots 211-42 (illus); Sotheby, 18 July 1985, lots 493-506 (43 coins, 14 illus.); Sotheby, 17 July 1986 lots 181-93; Glendining, 17 February 1988, lots 274-306 (77 coins, 15 illus., not stated to be from the hoard, but identical in composition).

[13] This last not in *MEC*, but 3 specimens from the July 1986 parcel are catalogued below, and two others were in the Glendining parcel of February 1988, lot 281.

English, the balance as between quantities of finds of that variety from England and the Continent ought to be discrepant; also, and more decisively, such a variety might be expected to show a greater than average concentration in the region of England where it was minted – Essex, Suffolk, Norfolk, Lincolnshire: if in England, it must have been minted specifically somewhere, and its origin ought to show up through comparisons of the various English distribution patterns for different sorts of porcupines.

Mapping the finds is the first method of attack. There are other, supplementary weapons in the numismatic armoury. Metrology may serve to show that two groups of coins were produced separately, either in time or place. Patterns of die-alignment may do the same, as may obverse:reverse die-ratios. Most statistical methods of handling the evidence rely, however, on the prior grouping of the coins by stylistic analysis.

Series D, Type 2c does not fall readily into stylistic groups, and metrology is correspondingly more important in its interpretation.

Type 8, which is much less plentiful than Type 2c (in the proportion one to 10 at Domburg, one to 10 in Aston Rowant, one to 4 among English site finds, and one to 45 at Remmerden) has a 'double reverse' design, combining the reverse of Type 2c with a simple 'standard' reverse. It is an obvious question to be asked, whether it is from the same mint as 2c, especially as its fabric is dissimilar, and it is virtually absent from Remmerden. The fact that the English ratio is out of line is not in itself sufficient, however, to indicate an English origin: the pattern seen in the English site-finds, which share the east-coast distribution of Type 2c, could equally well have arisen if Type 8 were Frisian, and accumulated in England, e.g. in the Aston Rowant hoard, through separate importation rather than via Domburg.

The classification of post-Aston Rowant porcupines is a massive task, but if they could be convincingly arranged into groups, a similar procedure could be followed. At least we have the confirmation of one large hoard and several smaller ones that the primary and secondary porcupines really are from distinct chronological phases, and that the hoards do not include numerous contemporary opportunistic copies of primary date.[14]

There are, finally, various scarce sceatta types which should be mentioned briefly, even though they have little bearing on the general

---

[14] *Catalogue des Deniers Mérovingiens de la Trouvaille de Bais (Ille-et-Vilaine)*, revised edition by J. Lafaurie, nos.309A and 309B are secondary porcupines, late additions to the catalogue from the Durocher collection, about which one may entertain a degree of doubt whether they are really from Bais.

problem of distinguishing the mint-places of Series D and E. There are copies of Series D, such as *BMC* Type 50, which are very possibly English. Vigilance for die-duplication or close stylistic similarities among English single finds may eventually reveal a few more. There are D/E 'mules' from English sites, which are probably English. And there are various independent types which copy the porcupine design of Series E. Series T, for example, is certainly English also. The '*Æthiliræd*' runic porcupines are also certainly English. Neither of these series is plentiful enough for its mint-place to be located with any confidence. They show, nevertheless, that copying of porcupines in England, outside the main minting centres, cannot be summarily dismissed from consideration.

The 'stepped cross' type, *BMC* Type 53, is more problematic. There are four or five English provenances, among two to three hundred porcupines, against only two from Domburg, among nearly five hundred. The numerical contrast is just enough to make a Domburg origin unlikely, but not, perhaps, an origin elsewhere in the Low Countries. For *BMC* Type 10, a D-related double-obverse type reading TILV, the numbers are even smaller, but a Low Countries origin seems assured by the Escharen hoard. The still scarcer 12/5 'mule', combining a London obverse with a porcupine reverse, is recorded only from the Low Countries, and presumably originated there, in spite of its English typology. When finds are so few, one has to calculate the statistical chances of even one specimen turning up, other than in a large find-assemblage. Negative evidence from anywhere other than Domburg may be merely an absence of evidence.

All these are minor, peripheral types. The big question that affects the outlines of monetary history is whether (as has been argued in the past[15]) the substantive varieties of porcupines were partly continental and partly English. By comparing sets of proportions at different sites or in different regions one can see clearly enough that in general they are continental. If any plentiful varieties were English, they should show up in the statistics, and in a degree of localization in England. One would be surprised if it were so.

Series D and E seem to be concurrent or at least overlapping types, each the distinctive currency of a major wic. E belongs to Dorestad, and D very probably to Domburg. The main outlines of an interpretation may need to be modified, however, to take account of copying at other mints – particularly, one suspects, in Frisia. Only when the Low

---

[15] Earlier views are summarized in D. M. Metcalf, 'A stylistic analysis of the "porcupine" sceattas', *NC*[7] 6 (1966), 179-205.

Countries finds have been fully published will it be possible to assess the style of all the specimens and to construct an accurate view of the stylistic groups. Progress is likely to be piecemeal. It will need to be located clearly within the perspectives of the general arguments that have been set out here.

THE CONTINENTAL RUNIC SCEATTAS
OF SERIES D, TYPE 2C

BMC Type 2c, the 'continental runic' type, is relatively much more plentiful at Domburg than at any other known site. It may have been minted there. Blackburn has suggested a dating to the years 700-15. The coins are mostly of excellent silver, but a few are sub-standard. Two weight-ranges can be recognized among the coins. The lighter kind average about three-quarters as much as the heavier. They have been seen as representing a later phase of the issue, following a devaluation. That is perhaps an anachronistic idea. Although the hoard evidence is ambiguous, it does not harmonize very well with an interpretation involving two phases. The hoards raise the question whether the lighter coins might not be contemporary copies, minted perhaps across the frontier in Frisian territory. The numismatist's most difficult problem is eventually to decide on the correct attribution of the lighter coins. If they were made with the intention of cheating or deceiving the users, it is possible that the normal rules of analysis of distribution patterns will not apply exactly. The coins may have been minted in Frisia, for the purpose of taking them to Domburg to spend, or of taking them to England to pass as decent Domburg coins.

There is plenty of material against which to test hypotheses: 189 site-finds from Domburg itself, and 15 or 20 more from various other sites in the Low Countries; 136 specimens in the Remmerden hoard, more than 160 in the Aston Rowant hoard, nearly fifty single finds from many different sites in England, and smaller but important groups in the Bais hoard and the Escharen hoard.

I

At their very best, the 'continental runic' sceattas copy the obverse of Type C2 so closely as to be virtually indistinguishable, and one might even wonder about purloined or transferred dies. Seriffing on the sloping bars of the runes *æ* and *a* is the only detail that arouses misgivings, in the case of the first coin catalogued below. When the runes are literate and carefully executed, they reproduce the *æpa* of Series C, never the inverted *epa* of the earliest variety of Series R. That probably reflects merely the date of introduction of Series D, and not trading links with a particular region of England. Very often, unfortunately, they are partly off the flan, and one cannot tell how accurate they are. On some specimens, however, they can be seen to consist of meaningless strokes linked together.

The simple, distinctive reverse design of cross pommee with pellets in the angles is surrounded by a pattern of pseudo-letters with a crosslet which (in accordance with later medieval convention) can be treated as an initial cross at 12 o'clock. Opposed to it there is a bold annulet at 6 o'clock. On either side the 'legend' is ΛVΛ ΛVΛ or something similar.

The best obverse style gives way almost immediately to rougher workmanship and stylistic diversity. There are no obvious runs of related dies, and no stylistic coherence. The material defies stylistic analysis. A seriffed initial cross is perhaps an early feature. It can be seen on the first coin catalogued below, and also on the specimen from the Birchington grave-find – which, from its place in the sequence of grave-finds, presumably belongs fairly early in Series D; although the plated specimen in the same find shows that forgery had already begun, with an A/D 'mule'.

Unexpectedly the reverse design, simple as it is, seems to offer easier prospects for the classification of Type 2c. The pelletted style (cross pommee) is sometimes replaced by a seriffed cross, or a sanserif cross. It may turn out that these are not straightforward criteria for grouping the coins, but at least they are likely to have been without significance at the time.

FIG. Series D, Type 2c. Two specimens from a find in the Kings Lynn area.

The two specimens of Type 2c in a find from the Kings Lynn area can be assigned a firm *terminus ante quem* from the English types in the find assuming they were associated. They are nondescript in style, with untidy reverses reminiscent of Type 8. The runes on one of the two read

185

æpp in rectangular lines of even thickness. The other coin is even further down the road of stylistic decline.

At the poorer end of the spectrum of style the face disintegrates into a few unrecognizable elements crushed between the remnants of the radiate crown and the truncation. The runes become illiterate or perfunctory. On a proportion of specimens the bust is laterally reversed. Constructing a corpus of Type 2c in the correct date order looks to be an almost impossible task, given the scarcity of die-linkage. It would be rash to assume that stylistic deterioration correlates at all closely with a chronological sequence.

In face of this utter confusion of style, the metrology of the type gives a first hint of order. The Bais hoard contained 17 specimens of Type 2c

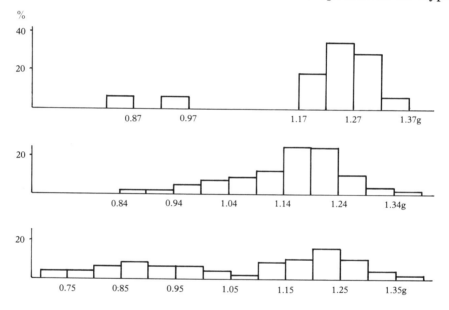

FIG. Weight patterns of Series D, Type 2c. Top: the Bais hoard (17 specimens). Middle: the Remmerden hoard (136 specimens). Bottom: the Aston Rowant hoard (a sample of 44 specimens). Note that these histograms are drawn to the same vertical and horizontal scales as those for the primary series, above, and that the value, e.g. 1.25g, is on the same vertical line in all three histograms.

already showing a wide stylistic diversity, but with a high average weight.[1] The modal value is 1.24g, with a compact distribution. (Note the

[1] M. Prou and E. Bougenot, *Catalogue des Deniers Méovingiens de la trouvaille de Bais (Ille-et-Vilaine)*, revised edition by J. Lafaurie, nos.311-18.

narrow step-interval of 0.05g). The two specimens below 1.18g were well below that figure, at 0.94 and 0.82g, and the second, in particular, was in a disintegrated obverse style. Three specimens with a tolerably accurate runic legend *æpa* or *apa* were among the heaviest, at 1.29, 1.28, and 1.28g.

The Remmerden hoard of 1988 provides a large sample of 136 coins,[2] with what appears to be a single peak at *c*.1.18g, although with some negative skewness which could be concealing a small proportion of specimens on a lower standard or standards. The modal value is lower than in the Bais hoard. It raises the question whether the earliest, and heaviest, coins had already begun to disappear from the currency – or whether perhaps Bais comprises coins specially selected for their fullness of weight.

The Escharen hoard of 1980[3] includes 5 specimens of Type 2c, weighing 1.20, 1.20, 1.15, 1.10, and 1.105g. They correspond with Remmerden as well as a small sample can be expected to do. The first four coins are coherent in style and of respectable workmanship, with more or less literate runes. Perhaps they reflect the output of a single workshop. The fifth coin is an obvious copy, for which there is a heavy die-duplicate in the Aston Rowant hoard.[4]

A sample of 44 specimens[5] from the Aston Rowant hoard shows some further downwards drift in the weights. The main peak of the histogram extends down to include the step 1.10-1.15g. There is also a clearly separate second peak, at about 0.9g. It might reflect a weight-reduction at the Domburg mint. Alternatively, the lighter coins may be from a separate source. Remmerden and Aston Rowant appear to be of very similar date of deposit. Both include porcupines of Variety G4. In Remmerden the sample of porcupines is very small, but in Aston Rowant it is large enough for the absence of varieties to be accepted as negative evidence. Unless Variety G came to an end well before the end of the early phase of porcupines, therefore, there is no room between the dates of deposit of Remmerden and Aston Rowant to accommodate a substantial second phase of Series D. If the style had been more accomplished and consistent, the products of two such mints would probably have been distinguishable by careful stylistic analysis. The chaotic impression that the type presents unfortunately makes it very difficult to recognize a stylistic discontinuity, or to reject the hypothesis

---

[2] Information kindly supplied by Mr. A. Pol.

[3] W. Op den Velde, 'Escharen 1980', *JMP* 72 (1985), 5-12.

[4] ibid.

[5] These are 36 coins in the 1988 auction sale, plus 8 coins now in the Ashmolean Museum, from the 1986 parcel.

that all the coins could be arranged into a single sequence. Nevertheless, the straightforward reading of the contrast between the two hoards is that the lighter variety of D is an imitative issue produced concurrently with the heavy coins, presumably at another mint-place. Remmerden will reflect a sum of money put together in territory from which the imitations were excluded, or perhaps a sum consisting of selected heavy coins; Aston Rowant will draw on both streams. It is desirable, obviously, to add some independent confirmation of this unexpected view of Series D, but how could one hope to do so?

If one could demonstrate a degree of stylistic coherence among the heavy group and similarly among the lighter group, what would that prove? – Merely that they were separate in terms of their production; but whether separate in time or place would remain more or less an open question, given the clumsiness of the obverse dies and the very easily reproduced design of the reverses.

Patterns of die-alignment offer no instant solution, although there are signs that the earliest coins are regularly die-adjusted.

It is a measure of the difficulty of finding proof that one should clutch at straws such as the two light coins in the Bais hoard, as possible evidence that coins on the lower weight-standard were already in existence at an early stage in the development of the heavier sequence – unless Bais is deceptive. We may have to wait until new hoards come to light.

II

A detailed examination of the alloy of Type 2c is full of interest, but it does not yield any useful criterion by which sheep may be separated from goats – nor, conversely, can it prove that the heavier and lighter coins are all sheep. Eight specimens from the Aston Rowant hoard, catalogued below, have been chemically analysed by EPMA, along with nine other coins of Type 2c in the Ashmolean collection. They show that about half the coins in the sample were of the highest purity, with 'silver' contents tightly clustered around 95-96 per cent. These coins contain no measurable amounts of tin. There are other specimens, however, which still have around 94-95 per cent 'silver', which contain 0.5-1.0 per cent tin. All but one of the specimens which fall below 92 per cent silver contain tin. The graph, plotting silver against tin, could fairly be said to show an inverse correlation, which may have some chronological implications (although one must allow for margins of uncertainty created

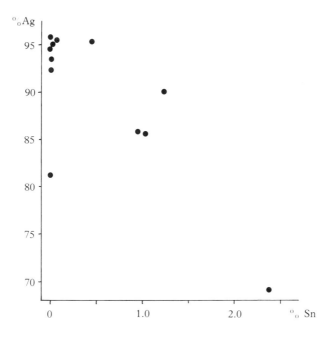

by tin enrichment as a result of corrosion, etc.). It may be that the tin-free coins, mostly of very pure silver, correspond with the earliest phase of Type 2c.

A correlation of silver contents against weight shows that coins in the lower weight-range could still be of very good silver.

Gold contents are high, and are very comparable with those of English primary sceattas. They show no clear trend against tin contents or against weight.

III

BMC Type 50 consists of a single coin (*BMC* 196). Its obverse type is not a chalice, but merely a crude copy of Type 2c. It is not necessarily English. Another coin somewhat reminiscent of it in style has been found at Wappenbury, Warwickshire.[6] The characteristic square C on the reverse shows that it is in fact a 2c/8 'mule', and therefore obviously imitative. Even a west midlands provenance is not, however, sufficient evidence of English origin. In order to make a case, two or three English

[6] 'Coin Register', 1988/111. When the late Bill Seaby first examined the coin, the obverse (seen upside down) made him think of a coffee-pot. Type 50, in the same vein, might be seen as a tea-pot.

stray finds in a related style, which does not occur at Domburg or in Remmerden, would be needed. The peripheral English provenance, in Warwickshire, attracts attention; but there is a normal specimen of Type

2c from nearby Bidford-on-Avon, which is from the same dies as an Aston Rowant coin catalogued below.

IV

There is a modern forgery of Type 2c, made from Wood's metal or one of a variety of similar fusible alloys composed of lead, tin, and bismuth.[7]

[7] D. M. Metcalf, 'Another modern forgery of a sceat', *BNJ* 48 (1978), 107; D. M. Metcalf and J. P. Northover, 'The Northumbrian royal coinage in the time of Æthelred II and Osberht', *Coinage in Ninth-Century Northumbria*, Oxford, 1987, 187-233, at pp.214f.

SERIES D, TYPE 8

SERIES D, Type 8 is a 'double-reverse' type which combines the cross-and-pellets reverse of Series D, Type 2c with a distinctive version of the standard reverse found on Series A, C, and E. Type 8 is much less plentiful than 2c, but it has a very similar distribution pattern, occurring at Domburg (1.8 per cent) and in the Aston Rowant hoard (c.5 per cent) and Remmerden hoard (2 per cent). There are about twenty single finds from England, with a scattered East Anglian and east-coast distribution which is indistinguishable from that of Type 2c. It is natural to assume that Type 8 is another continental issue, quite closely related to Type 2c.

It is unlikely on grounds of style to be from the same mint-place as Type 2c, with which the hoards show it to be roughly contemporary. The pseudo-legend around the cross-and-pellets motif is different in detail from that on 2c, and is quite consistent. The best specimens are of very pure, tin-free silver, and on the highest continental weight-standard, suggesting a date of origin close to that of 2c. There does not seem to be sufficient room, before the date of deposit of the Aston Rowant and Remmerden hoards, for 2c and 8 to have been successive issues from the same mint. – At least, if that had been the case, traces might have been detectable in the hoard evidence.

In the last resort, nevertheless, the only direct way to demonstrate that Type 8 and 2c were from different mints would be to show that their distribution-patterns on the Continent were divergent. That is still impossible, because there is far too little local evidence.

One is searching, in practice, for discrepancies in the ratio of Type 8 to 2c, in comparison with the same ratio at Domburg and in the major hoards. At Domburg 18 specimens of Type 8 have been reported, as against 189 of Type 2c – a ratio of about 1 to 10. The figure is very similar in the Aston Rowant hoard, but in Remmerden it is 1 to 45. Type 8, in other words, was virtually excluded from Remmerden, along with reduced-weight specimens of 2c. The three specimens that yield the ratio of 1:45 can be looked upon as strays, accidentally retained in the hoard. If Remmerden is seen as a traveller's hoard reflecting the currency close

MAPS. Single finds of Series D. Left: Type 2c (46 specimens, including 8 from near Bedford and at least 6 from Tilbury). Right: Type 8 (17 specimens, including 2 each from North Ferriby, Royston, and Tilbury). Type 8Z (square symbol).

to the (official) mint of Type 2c, that will perhaps amount to an argument that Type 8 is from elsewhere.

Type 8, curiously, is relatively plentiful among the English single-finds, where the ratio is about 1 to 3. One's first thought is to wonder whether it could be an English derivative of 2c; or whether the English ratio could be distorted by the inclusion of local copies of a continental type. That needs to be explored by comparing the range of style among the English single finds, with the range seen at Domburg. Another explanation for the high ratio might be that Type 8 was carried to England preferentially. That need not imply that its mint-place was more accessible to the east coast of England than Domburg (which is difficult to envisage); it could be a preference arising out of the terms of trade or the balance of payments.

192

FIG. Series D, Type 8. From a find in the Kings Lynn area.

The recent Kings Lynn find included one specimen of Type 8 and two of 2c. It is of value as being only a year or two later in date than Aston Rowant, in which the ratio was very different.

Against that general statistical background the single finds recovered beneath the sand-dunes at De Panne, (near Coxyde) few as they are, take on new interest. They comprised 3 specimens of 2c, 3 specimens of 8, 4 porcupines of Variety G, and 2 coins of Series G.[1] The ratio, based admittedly on very small numbers, is one to one, in a find-assemblage which appears to be solidly from the early eighth century.

The Aquitanian hoards contribute their mite. In Saint-Pierre-les-Etieux there was one coin of Type 8 and 2 of Type 2c; and in Plassac one of each. But the Bais hoard, from Britanny, shows a 1:17 ratio, with heavy coins of Type 2c.

The best guess we can make is that Type 8 is from a mint-place lying a little way south-west of Domburg, on the Belgian coast, or alternatively perhaps in the upper Meuse valley. There is no reason to suspect a location any further west: Type 8 reached England by way of the North Sea trade, and it is absent from Hamwic and the south coast generally. If its place of origin happens to be a blank on our map of finds, there is nothing we can do to remedy the deficiency.

I

In place of the pseudo-legend +ΛVΛOΛVΛ which is standard on Type 2c, Type 8 has fewer symbols, untidily disposed, and often including a large

Ɩ (usually facing inwards), a clear A, and/or a diamond-shaped O and a large N or H with sloping cross-bar. The style is pommee. The untidiness

[1] W. Op den Velde, W. J. de Boone, and A. Pol, 'A survey of sceatta finds from the Low Countries', in *Sceattas in England and on the Continent*, pp.117-45 at p.143.

is such that it is unusual to find pellets regularly disposed in all four quarters of the cross.

The standard type has four L-shaped elements around the central annulet (which sometimes encloses a pellet), or 3 Ls and an I (possibly the earlier version?). The L symbol has a pellet at the angle, sometimes inconspicuous. When the detail is on the flan, the outer border seems always to be regularly organized, the complete pattern consisting of a tufa at the top (borrowed from Type C1?), an Λ enclosing a pellet below, and crosses at the sides.

The heaviest coins of this description weigh anything from *c.*1.20 to *c.*1.30g. They are 93-96 per cent 'silver', with 1.0-1.5 parts of gold, and with no tin. The least distinctive of the regular coins catalogued below still weighs 1.21g but is only 87 per cent silver, with a trace of tin.

There are other, much lighter specimens of thinner fabric and finer (although very blundered) engraving. Paradoxically they have four pellets neatly placed in the angles of the cross. One which is catalogued below weighs only 0.62g and is in fact a plated forgery on a copper core. It comes from the Aston Rowant hoard, which contained at least one die-duplicate weighing 0.87g. The Domburg find, Dirks pl.F, 20, is possibly another.

II

The English single finds, so far as photographs are available from which they can be checked, are mostly in regular style.[2] The London (Maiden Lane) and Lakenheath finds are from the same dies.[3]

Imitations and derivative coins are readily recognized. There is a variant on which the cross-and-pellets is replaced by cross-and-annulets. The four annulets are large, with a lightly indicated pellet at the centre. North Ferriby 5 is an example, and there is another from extremely similar if not the same dies, from Tilbury.[4] The North Ferriby coin weighs only 0.77g.

Royston 8 is patently imitative, with a T O T - - reverse.

[2] The following seem to be of acceptable style: Bedford 1.17g, Birchington, Colchester, Knaresborough, Lakenheath, London (Maiden Lane), North Ferriby 6, Thwing (cf. the Lelewel coin), and Tilbury (2 specimens).

[3] P. Stott, 'Saxon and Norman coins from London', in A. G. Vince (editor), *Aspects of Saxon and Norman London. 2. Finds and Environmental Evidence*, 1991 at pp.279-325, no.10 (illus.), and Lakenheath photo, pers.comm. Mr. Ron Morley (finder).

[4] E. J. E. Pirie, 'Some Northumbrian finds of sceattas', in *Sceattas in England and on the Continent*, pp.207-215, at p.208, and Fig.10. Tilbury photo, pers.comm. Mr. M. J. Bonser.

III

A much simplified derivative, which deserves a separate label (Type 8Z?), is without any legend. It is scarce, but has now been recorded in the

Aston Rowant hoard (1.24g), a die-duplicate from Cobham Park, Kent (1.26g), and Great Bircham, Norfolk (1.20g).[6] A Domburg find mules the same simplified standard reverse with an unusual version of the porcupine design.[7]

If both categories of imitation are set aside, the ratio of Type 8 to 2c among the English finds falls to about 1 to 4. That is still very different from Domburg.

IV

A coin of Type 8 which was engraved by Lelewel has been the subject of modern forgery.[8] The specimen illustrated in the catalogue, below, is of modern silver, largely free from the minor constituents and trace elements found in eighth-century silver. It must have been cast from a genuine coin, however, for the same cross-and-pellets die is represented in the Ashmolean collection by a coin from Aston Rowant, which has also been analysed, and which is certainly authentic.

[6] Blackburn and Bonser, ibid., p.84, no.93 (Great Bircham) and 93B (Aston Rowant). Illus.93c, on plate 5, is not referred to in the text. For Cobham Park, see 'Coin Register', BNJ 58 (1988), no.109, where the illustration is transposed with no.130 and appears on pl.38.

[7] Blackburn and Bonser, line drawing reproduced as 93A.

[8] D. M. Metcalf and L. K. Hamblin, 'A modern forgery of a sceat', BNJ 37 (1968), 190-1.

SERIES E: THE FOUR EARLY VARIETIES
OF PORCUPINES

A STYLISTIC analysis of the porcupines published in 1966 showed that there were a dozen different versions of the reverse design, each of which correlated with an equally distinctive version of the obverse. That the versions are separate blocks of coinage in terms of their minting is to some extent confirmed by the unimportant detail of the ornaments added in the border of the reverse, outside the square of the standard – which, again, correlate well.[1] The analysis of 1966 was far from comprehensive: the majority of porcupines do not fit into any of the categories. It would have been more accurate to speak of a stylistic analysis of the early and the late porcupines.

The problem was greatly clarified by the discovery, in 1971, of the Aston Rowant hoard, which contained at least seventy early porcupines, of just four substantive varieties, in fairly equal quantities.[2] In terms of the 1966 analysis, these were D, G, J, and another which was discussed, but not assigned a place in the alphabetical scheme: it was referred to as the 'VOIC' variety, because the reverse seemed to be attempting an inscription made up of those four letters. More recently, students have preferred to read VICO. The Aston Rowant hoard is large enough, and varied enough, for us to be reasonably certain that at its date of concealment, c.705-10, no other substantive varieties were yet in production. The early development of Series E, up to that date, is the story of those four varieties, and it needs to be understood in terms of the relationships between them.

As regards the moment of origin of Series E, an absence of evidence may or may not amount to negative evidence. The absence of porcupines from the English grave-finds (other than from one recent find from the Kings Lynn area) is not conclusive proof that their introduction post-dates the availability, in their home region, of Series C. The grave-finds are numerically small, and may be selective. If, however, Series C (rather

---

[1] D. M. Metcalf, 'A stylistic analysis of the "porcupine" sceattas', *NC*[7] 6 (1966), 179-205.

[2] J. P. C. Kent, in *Oxoniensia* 37 (1972), 243f.; *Coin Hoards* 1 (1975), 87.

than A) was the prototype, as the reverse border ornaments suggest, the porcupines will not begin until *c*.695. The four varieties therefore have to be accommodated in a period of about ten or at most about fifteen years.

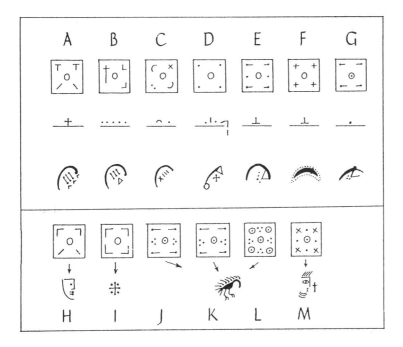

The question 'where' has received almost as many answers as there are scholars who have addressed it. The article of 1966 saw the substantive varieties as being from different regions, and reached the specific conclusion that D, J, and 'VICO' were English. (Variety G was left unassigned to any minting region.) In 1984 the writer retracted that opinion and accepted four arguments which together suggested that the early porcupines belonged, after all, to the region of the Rhine mouths.[3] These were that

1) iconographically they were far removed from the repertoire of designs that had been used for English coins up to the date of their introduction;

2) on the whole it seemed that a distinctive design served as the emblem of each particular mint or region or kingdom in England;

[3] D. M. Metcalf, 'Monetary circulation in southern England in the first half of the eighth century', in *Sceattas in England and on the Continent*, pp.27-69, at p.32.

3) there was no English region within the zone marked out by the majority of finds of primary sceattas, to which the porcupines could convincingly be assigned, for if they had been minted in Kent, Essex, Middle Anglia, or Mercia, one might have expected to be able to detect some signs of it in their distribution – as one can, for example, in the case of the undoubtedly English porcupine derivative in the secondary phase, Series T;

4) the degree of stylistic development within the early varieties pointed to their having been minted over quite a long period, possibly two or three decades. In other words, they looked like substantive issues, from a quite important mint or mints.

Those four arguments reflect a general response to the early porcupines, as viewed (it might be said) through English eyes. They remain valid as a context for more rigorous arguments based on comparisons of the proportions of porcupines from different sites and regions.

It has been argued in a preceding section that the porcupines as a whole are associated with Dorestad and with the area of the Rhine mouths. To describe them as Frisian, and thus to associate them with a race of men well known as merchants and seafarers, may be historically correct, but at the same time politically misleading. Dorestad lay close to, but usually within the frontiers of Merovingian power. In terms of social history and settlement, there was doubtless a strong Frisian presence extending some way south of the frontier.

Because they are a frontier coinage, it is also possible that porcupines were imitated beyond the frontier, in Frisia proper.

The 47 per cent representation of the series among the site-finds at Dorestad, and equally at Domburg, shows conclusively that the porcupines are continental. The over-all statistics are dominated, however, by secondary porcupines. Can we be absolutely sure, in a matter that has been long disputed, that the primary or early porcupines are likewise continental? Was the analysis of 1966 diametrically in error?

The early percentages, after all, point the other way. Instead of an over-all 47 per cent at Dorestad and Domburg, against 21 per cent in England, we find 6 per cent at Domburg[4] (and a roughly comparable figure in the much smaller sample of finds from Dorestad etc.) against 8 per cent in England; and not a few of the specimens which make up the 6 per cent at Domburg appear to be imitative.

[4] This figure is based on the researches of Dr. W. Op den Velde, to whom I am indebted for information in advance of publication.

Yet it would be an extravagant hypothesis to suggest that the distinctive porcupine design originated in England (where in England?), and then migrated to the Rhine mouths. It is not impossible, but the evidence would have to be very clear in order to overcome the handicap with which such an idea started out. It would seem even more extravagant to propose that just one of the four early varieties was from elsewhere than Dorestad. Yet the suggestion has been made that Variety D, which has been found in northern France and in the Hampshire basin, had a more westerly origin. Although that is at first sight implausible, it is only in the last few years that new evidence has made it possible to argue against the hypothesis. Similarly, one may still reasonably ask oneself whether the 'plumed bird' variety (that is, Variety J), with its very distinctive modification of the iconography of the porcupine type, could be English. It is relatively much more plentiful in England (compared with Domburg) than the other three varieties. Could it be the odd man out?[5] It seems not, for the origin of the design (discussed below) requires us to believe that the 'plumed birds' and Variety G belong together.

The archaeological approach to the question is to repeat, on a smaller scale, the argument by which the porcupines as a whole are shown to be continental. For the four early varieties, the evidence, as already indicated, is at first sight ambiguous. If they are relatively more plentiful in England than at Domburg (and probably, even, than at Dorestad), that seems to imply very large outflows of money from the Rhine mouths area to England. In the secondary phase, quite different conditions obtained. The facts can best be grasped by comparing the 6 per cent and 41 per cent respectively of primary and secondary porcupines at Domburg – a ratio of one to about seven – with the corresponding ratio in England of one to about one and a half. Putting it in that way shows that it is not simply a question of the English monetary economy expanding, under an initial impetus from Frisian trade. Either the outflows from Dorestad dwindled, or most of the secondary porcupines reaching England were reminted into English secondary types.

The same argument from relative proportions could in principle be repeated in miniature separately for each of the four varieties, but it runs into statistical imprecision, as the numbers in the samples become smaller. Such discrepancies as exist may well be fortuitous, lying within the relatively wider margins of statistical error.

Small-scale comparisons are made even more vague by the difficulty of

---

[5] For the hypothesis of a westerly origin for Variety D, see D. M. Metcalf, 'A "porcupine" sceat from Market Lavington, with a list of other sceattas from Wiltshire', *Wiltshire Archaeological Magazine* 83 (1990), 205-8. For statistics relating to the 'plumed bird' variety, see the table below.

making appropriate allowance for imitations, which may distort the proportions in ways that are difficult to understand and allow for.

Another line of argument which tends to show that the early porcupines are continental in origin is provided by mapping the English finds – something which can now be done more fully even than in 1984. The argument set out under 3) above still stands: the early porcupines are found so widely that they are unlikely to be English. Their distribution can be seen to contrast with that of the English primary series – although it must be admitted that the differences are not dramatic, for the English primary sceattas, too, moved about very freely and are sometimes found at considerable distances from their place of origin. Nevertheless each English primary type tends to have a region, within its wider pattern of distribution, where it is relatively more abundant, and makes up a greater share of all the primary finds from the region. That seems not to be true of the porcupines in England. Rather, finds from as far apart as Yorkshire, Lincolnshire, Kent, and Hampshire suggest that they came ashore at many different localities, having been carried by sea from the Rhine mouths area.

A similarly wide distribution was achieved, nevertheless, by Series G and J, in the first case apparently from a north French place of origin, and in the second as a result of multiple origins, in Yorkshire and Frisia. The careful topographical analysis of a large body of find-material is needed in order to overcome these uncertainties, because it seems that the spread of sceattas from quite different places could generate superficially quite similar patterns of finds. Even so, we can reiterate our conviction that, by c.695-710, there were few if any vacant regions in southern or eastern England to which English types have not already been attributed; and that if the early porcupines had been minted anywhere in the south or east, their region of origin would almost certainly be discoverable through a relative concentration of finds in that region – and it seems not to be. We are, after all, looking for the origins not of some small or ephemeral issue, but of a large series, in which die-duplication is scarce.

When it comes to applying the same distributional arguments to each of the four early varieties separately, the case ought in some ways to be a stronger one, because comparisons allow us to discount most of the uncertainties. But it has only recently begun to be possible to escape the statistical uncertainties attaching to small samples, as the English find-evidence has grown in strength. All four show a widespread distribution, but there are minor differences between them which may or may not be significant. Thus Variety D is almost absent from the south-east; and

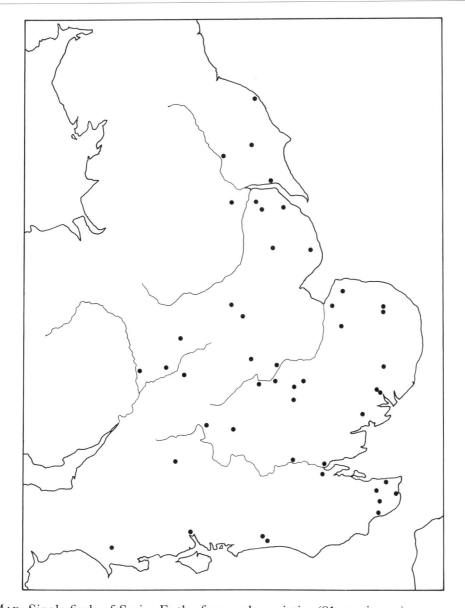

MAP. Single finds of Series E: the four early varieties (81 specimens).

MAPS. Single finds of Series E. Left: 'plumed bird' varieties (23 specimens, including 4 from Hamwic, 3 from Reculver, 3 from Royston). Right: the VICO variety (15 specimens).

VICO is absent at Southampton. If one of the four varieties were English or north French, for example, could one tell from this set of maps? Is the distribution of 'plumed birds' (i.e. Varieties J/K and L) more like that of Series G than a North-Sea, east-coast distribution? It must be admitted that the evidence is not so clear-cut that the idea can be dismissed out of hand. 'Plumed birds' are conspicuous at Hamwic, where their typology is echoed at a later date by Series H, Type 49 (annulets or crosses under the bird's neck). Mules with the reverse type of Series G also hint at a westerly zone of circulation: they are known from the Cimiez hoard.

One further complication of the English evidence: selective processes may have operated, distorting the expected geographical spread of the porcupines. In particular they may have penetrated more easily into regions which were short of currency, or which lacked their own issues. That might partly explain their occurrence north of the Wash, and also

MAPS. Single finds of Series E. Left: Variety G (34 specimens). Right: Variety D (9 specimens).

perhaps at Hamwic in the earliest years after the town was laid out.

We turn now to a narrower consideration of the question 'where'. Granted that the early porcupines are from the Rhine mouths area, are they all from the same wic or mint-place? Could each be from a separate trading centre on the distributaries of the Rhine? It is after all curious that several distinctive designs should have been minted alongside each other, each being struck from a considerable number of dies and retaining its identity through a process of stylistic devolution. The English distributional evidence is of no help in resolving this difficulty: by the time the early porcupines had been carried from the Rhine mouths area to England, and lost, they were already well mixed.

Were there three or four moneyers at Dorestad, each striking sceattas independently in his own workshop? Did the varieties originate at different dates? They were all circulating together in c.705-10 when the

Aston Rowant hoard was concealed, and their minting, as well as their use, must have been partly concurrent. Dorestad was certainly the dominant port of the Rhine distributaries by the third quarter of the eighth century. How dominant it was at the end of the seventh century is less certain. (Dendrochronological evidence from the harbour excavations hardly goes earlier than 700, but we should remember the Madelinus tremisses.) The four varieties are too evenly balanced (Varieties G and VICO both being plentiful) to allow us to imagine that the varieties could be from a cluster of mint-places on the Lek and the Waal, with just one dominant variety attributable to Dorestad.

The straightforward procedure for distinguishing between Dorestad and nearby wics would be to compare percentages at different local sites. Because the porcupines no doubt enjoyed a lively circulation in the Rhine mouths area, such a procedure would only be practicable if there were big series of finds from a good number of sites, including the production-sites of each variety. Such evidence does not exist. We are heavily dependent on finds from the two major sites, namely Domburg (with its magnificent assemblage of a thousand sceattas) and Dorestad (with a mere sixty). For Dorestad, the presumed home of the early porcupines, the sample is so tiny as to be virtually useless. Even if we include the well-published finds from nearby Maurik and Rijswijk,[6] we cannot do much more than establish the ratio of early to secondary porcupines.

The relationship of the four varieties therefore remains puzzling, and our only course of action is to test the nul hypothesis in as many ways as we can, on the chance of finding significant differences between them. Clues to the relationship of the four varieties may lie in their weight patterns and alloy standards. All four are heavy, with modal values in the region of 1.20-1.30g. 'VICO' and Variety G sometimes exceed 1.30g. There is some falling away from the best levels, particularly in Variety D. All four are also initially of excellent silver, commonly 95 or 96 per cent, with occasional falling away. Any metrological differences, in short, arc so slight that large and carefully controlled samples would be needed to demonstrate them. Their gold contents (0.9 to 1.4 parts per hundred) are comparable, and they are almost all tin-free.

Mules would of course be informative, but what we find appear rather to be imitative pieces (although often of respectable weight and alloy), particularly G/VICO 'mules'. These cannot be assumed to tell us anything about the relationship of the regular varieties, except that they were both familiar to the copiers – whose workshops will not necessarily have been

[6] W. Op den Velde, 'Sceatta's gevonden bij Maurik en Rijswijk', *JMP* 69 (1962), 5-19.

in Dorestad or even on the Continent.

Comparisons between hoards and site-finds are another possible line of enquiry. It will be in order to look for any differences in the proportions of the four varieties between the English single finds and the Aston Rowant hoard, on the grounds that the former will have been lost gradually over a relatively longer period, whereas the latter may well reflect the somewhat tighter age-structure of the porcupine population at the date of the hoard's concealment – and may even reflect money recently imported to England. The English single finds and the Domburg finds should afford a straight comparison, as both will have been lost piece-meal in much the same way.

If there were another large hoard, from a decade or so earlier than Aston Rowant, and standing close to the date of origin of the porcupines, it would almost certainly be illuminating, both for the chronological relationship of the four varieties, and for the stylistic development within each. There is, alas, no such hoard. Those that are available contain only a few porcupines. Saint-Pierre-les-Etieux[7] and Bais[8] have 4 and 8 respectively. Remmerden has 5.[9] The first two are from distant find-spots, and in all three the porcupines form only a small minority of strays, in a sum made up of other types. That puts a question-mark against their reliability as evidence.

Provisionally, the basic statistics are as follows (coins, *not* percentages):

TABLE 2. *Occurrence of the four early varieties of porcupines in various hoards, site-finds, etc.*

	Aston Rowant	English finds	Domburg finds[10]	Saint-Pierre	Remmerden	Bais
'Plumed bird'	5	20	9	-	-	-
VICO	34	15	18	1	2	(2)
G	21	32	24	3	3	2
D	12	6	12	-	-	-

[7] J. Lafaurie, ' Monnaies d'argent mérovingiennes des VIIe et VIIIe siècles: les trésors de Saint-Pierre-les-Etieux (Cher), Plassac (Gironde), et Nohanet (Puy-de-Dôme),' *RN*⁶ 11 (1969), 98-219.

[8] J. Lafaurie, *Catalogue des deniers Mérovingiens de la trouvaille de Bais (Ille-et-Vilaine)* (2nd edition, revised, of a study by M. Prou and E. Bougenot).

[9] I am indebted for information and photographs in advance of publication by Arent Pol.

[10] Statistics by courtesy of Dr. Op den Velde.

'Plumed birds', which are unexpectedly well represented in the Hamwic excavations, seem to be under-represented in Aston Rowant, where the **VICO** variety is over-represented. Otherwise the differences, including the absences, appear to be within the limits of statistical variation.

I

The derivation of the 'porcupine' design has been much discussed, generally in terms of the deformation of a profile bust. The truth is even stranger than the many theories. Dhénin, in his study, 'Homotypies anachroniques',[11] had the pleasure of solving this long-standing problem.

FIG. Prototypes of early porcupines, of Variety G and the 'plumed bird' variety: bronze coins of the Carnutes (after Dhénin, Figs. 8 and 10).

In the context of other examples of the copying of Celtic coin-types, he argued convincingly that Variety G of the early porcupines is closely copied from a bronze coin of the Carnutes, and that the 'plumed bird' is copied from the eagle on the reverses of the same series. Strange as this claim is, seeing that the coins of the Carnutes did not circulate as far afield as the Rhine mouths area (nor in England), Dhénin's illustrations of the parallels are extremely persuasive. As there is a similar case in the sceattas of Series K, there can be no doubt that such copying happened. The palm goes to Dhénin, therefore. As he permits himself to remark, 'Il y a souvent à de grands mystères des petites réponses'.

The connection, through the bronze of the Carnutes, between Variety G and the 'plumed bird' variety demonstrates a common origin, and thereby rules out the possibility that the latter is English.

II

The 'plumed bird' sceattas fall essentially into two groups, with very

[11] M. Dhénin, 'Homotypies anachroniques', *Mélanges offerts au docteur J.-B. Colbert de Beaulieu*, 1987, pp.311-13.

different reverse types, and with corresponding symbols under the bird's neck – a cross pommee associated with reverse variety J/K, and an annulet with central pellet associated with Variety L. Variety J was represented in the Aston Rowant hoard, but not, apparently, K or L.[12] The less plentiful Variety L is probably absent because it is later in date than Aston Rowant, although the sample is very small to warrant the conclusion. The Hallum hoard contained one specimen each of J and L.[13]

The later dating of Variety L is in any case supported by metrology. It is lighter than J/K, and it may also be of less fine silver. The change in design may even have been adopted to mark a change in intrinsic value.

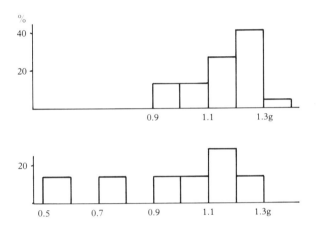

FIG. Weight patterns of Series E, 'plumed bird' varieties. Top: Varieties J/K (22 specimens). Bottom: Variety L (7 specimens). There is no obvious systematic difference in the sources of the two groups of specimens; the patterns would seem, therefore, to reflect a real difference. Note that the step-interval is 0.1g, giving a much more favourable impression of the accuracy of the type than the histograms of primary series and Series D, above. The various early and secondary porcupines, however, are all plotted using the same horizontal scale, with a step-interval of 0.1g, and are thus visually directly comparable.

Variety J/K has a modal weight of c.1.25g, with a rather skew distribution. Variety L, on the basis of only a small sample, is poorly controlled. There need be little doubt that it is later than J/K. The evidence of silver contents is less useful. Three specimens catalogued below, all of Variety J, contain 96, 96, and 93 per cent 'silver'. Another,

[12] J. P. C. Kent, in *Oxoniensia* 1972, records only one specimen of *BMC* Type 6, of variety J. Glendining, 13 March 1975, lot 237; Glendining, 17 February 1988, lots 287-88.
[13] Dirks, pl.C, 12 and 15, and p.57.

somewhat corroded, from Hamwic is estimated at 89 per cent. A specimen of Variety L in Cardiff is 88 per cent silver, with a very small addition of tin.[14]

There are two quite different styles of bird, one with a rounded, naturalistic body and curved neck, the other with a tubular body from which the neck is continued as a straight line, before making a right-angled bend. These styles correlate imperfectly with the varieties: J/K coins mostly have naturalistic birds, and L mostly tubular. But there are exceptions in both groups, of coins which are perfectly acceptable in

FIG. 'Plumed bird' variety. Specimens with rounded body, with tubular body, and with numerous quills.

style. There may have been two die-cutters working side by side. A rearrangement of the type to make the shape of the bird's body the main criterion for chronology is ruled out by the pattern of weights.

Another variable feature of the coins' style is found in the number of quills, which are sometimes tightly packed. All in all, the stylistic variation among the 'plumed birds', and the scarcity of die-links,[15] point to a considerable output over a period of time.

The formal difference between Varieties J and K is small: the triangles of pellets are inverted. Some specimens have one of each arrangement, and others have the three dots in a straight line. These tend to lack the cross pommee under the bird's neck, having instead a row of three pellets, or a line terminated by pellets, or a defective cross. On the same specimens one can usually see the cross in front of the bird's head, which otherwise tends to be off the flan or perhaps even omitted.[16] If we take into account their accurate weights, we may suppose that the irregular J/K coins are early and experimental.

BMC 74, found at Reculver in the eighteenth century, mixes the formal elements of the designs of J/K and L: it has a pelletted annulet under the neck, associated with reverse K. Its general style is perfectly acceptable, and its weight is high.[17] One should hesitate to think of it as transitional.

[14] Hamwic 4; NMW E.010, ex Lockett 222a.

[15] The Six Hills find is from the same obverse as *BMC* 73.

[16] Six Hills has three dots in a row. Wharram Percy, and a very similar specimen among the Roach Smith London finds, have a line.

[17] *BMC* 74 = *NC* 1966, pl.15, 17 = Stowe 16, 1.23g.

Another irregular specimen, Royston 12, Variety J, replaces the cross pommee with a group of three pellets. For good measure, the same ornament is repeated between the bird's legs and again behind its legs. The naturalistic bird is plump. The coin's weight is at the top of the range. Its place in the scheme is, however, a little uncertain.

The Aston Rowant specimens referred to above have a scrawny 'naturalistic' bird, with reverse J. At least one of them has a second cross pommee, behind the bird's legs and below its tail.

Hamwic 4, 5, and 6, also formally of variety J, are stylistically very close to each other, and they are not very similar to the Aston Rowant coins. The cross pommee under the neck is replaced by a cruciform group of four bold pellets. The whole style is deeply and coarsely cut, with large pellets. The similarity of the Hamwic finds is intriguing. They

FIG. 'Plumed bird' variety. Hamwic 4 and 5.

look as if they came from the same batch of the mint's output. Three coins are hardly a valid statistical sample, but they should not be lost sight of, because they speak against any hypothesis that the 'plumed birds' could be English, specifically an early Hamwic issue. A similar specimen comes from a collection formed in Winchester in the eighteenth century.[18] It is the only sceat in the collection, and one wonders whether it may not have been a Hamwic find, reinforcing the idea of a batch of coinage which entered the currency of the new town very soon after it was laid out.

Variety L includes pairs of coins with 'tubular' and plump-bodied naturalistic birds, linked by very similar reverse dies,[19] which strongly suggest that both styles were being produced concurrently.

Variety L apparently tails off into specimens on which the groups of pellets between the annulets on the reverse, instead of being in threes, are reduced to twos or single pellets. The Marston find, from near Oxford,[20] is an example. Chipped, it weighs 0.74g.

Cimiez 61 is probably another, which is of full weight (1.25g). It is

---

[18] *SCBI Yorkshire* 941.

[19] *NC* 1966, pl.15, nos.19 and 20, and nos.21 and 22.

[20] D. M. Metcalf, 'Twenty-five notes on sceatta finds', in *Sceattas in England and on the Continent*, pp.193-205, at p.194 and pl.10, 2.

FIG. 'Plumed bird' variety. Marston find.

difficult to be sure where one should draw the line, however, between the (presumed) tail-end of Variety L, and imitations. Domburg 199[21] is not unlike the Marston find except that the bird is laterally reversed. The coin's find-spot perhaps speaks against its being official. Over Royston 15, another rough specimen of Variety L, one need not hesitate. The reverse has pellets in threes and singly, with strange thick lines in the outer border. The bird has only one clumsy leg, and its plumes lie the wrong way. Beneath the neck is an unpelleted annulet, but also a group of three pellets. The tail feathers are untidy.

The scatter of finds in the east midlands and north which fit into the stylistic scheme that has been outlined – Wharram Percy,[22] North Ferriby,[23] Crosby,[24] Six Hills,[25] Melton Mowbray,[26] St.Neots,[27] Royston 12 and 14,[28] and Marston – allow us to feel confident that we understand what the official 'plumed birds' should look like. The assemblage of finds is relatively free from imitations, Royston 15 being an exception. Three finds from Reculver tally.[29]

That consistency helps to show that the group of 'plumed birds' from Cimiez is eccentric.[30] Cimiez 57 is a 'mule' of the 'plumed bird' obverse

FIG. 'Plumed bird' variety, imitations. Cimiez 57, 58, and 59.

[21] *NC* 1966, pl.15, 24.

[22] Information by courtesy of Miss E. J. E. Pirie.

[23] E. J. E. Pirie, 'Some Northumbrian finds of sceattas', in *Sceattas in England and on the Continent*, pp.207-215, no.8 and pl.11, 13.

[24] The illustration in D. M. Metcalf, 'Monetary affairs in Mercia in the time of Æthelbald', in *Mercian Studies*, edited by A. Dornier, Leicester, 1977, p.95, Fig.9 has a reverse which mixes J and K, and a defective cross under the neck.

[25] Blackburn and Bonser, 'Single finds – 2', *BNJ*

55 (1985), no.61, from the same obv. as *BMC* 73 and a very similar rev.

[26] id., 'Single finds – 1', *BNJ* 54 (1984), no.20.

[27] *MEC* 655.

[28] M. A. S. Blackburn and M. J. Bonser, 'Finds from a Middle Anglian site near Royston, Herts.', in 'Single finds of Anglo-Saxon and Norman coins – 3', *BNJ* 56 (1986), 65-80.

[29] *BMC* 74; *MEC* 653; *MEC* 654.

[30] P. le Gentilhomme, 'La circulation des sceattas dans la Gaule mérovingienne', *RN* 1938, pl.4.

with the TOT/II reverse of a secondary porcupine. It is patently imitative. Nos.58 and 59 mule the 'tubular' and naturalistic birds respectively with the reverse of Series G. The obverse of no.58 is in very competent style, and if it were not keeping such disreputable company, one might not venture to exclude it from the main series. Cimiez 60 and another similar coin in Paris have lightly engraved reverses, but seem acceptable as specimens of Variety J. No.61 has already been mentioned as a late example of Variety L. No.62 is clumsy, and may be by the same hand as no.59. The Morel-Fatio collection in fact contained ten 'plumed birds', the published weights of which [31] do not match up with the six published by Le Gentilhomme.

Among the more exotic imitations may be mentioned a Series D/'plumed bird' (var.K) 'mule' from Bawsey, catalogued below.

Nothing in the detailed evidence offers any support for the hypothesis that the 'plumed bird' sceattas are English or north French, although the Cimiez hoard may reflect some French copying. The English single finds, particularly those from the east midlands and the north, point to imports via the North Sea trade, probably with a bias towards those regions of England that were under-supplied with currency in the years around 700. Variety L may turn out to have a distribution that reaches further inland; and the Hamwic finds are perhaps a special case.

Series H may well echo the symbols of the 'plumed birds', if the latter had become familiar in circulation at Hamwic, but that does not prove anything about their place of origin.

III

The square banner of the standard on the porcupines is copied from English sceattas of Series A or C. The use of crosses in the margins suggests C as the more likely prototype, in which case the English coins may provide a *terminus ante quem non*. The votive inscription in the banner is replaced, on the early porcupines, either by a simpler geometrical design, or in one variety by an arrangement of symbols which, with the help of imagination, one may see as made up of the letters VICO[32] – a familiar Merovingian coin legend which would be very appropriate to the coinage of a *wic*, although a *vicus* need not be that. The

---

[31] A. Morel-Fatio and A. Chabouillet, *Catalogue raisonné de la collection de deniers mérovingiens des VIIe et VIIe siècles de la trouvaille de Cimiez*, 1890, no.323.

[32] The coins were formerly described as VOIC, because of a specimen reading VOI in the margin (*NC* 1966, pl.15, 10. It was Dr. Kent who perceptively suggested VICO.

variety is in any case conveniently labelled the 'VICO' variety. Its reverse stands out at such an early date, from the more usual symmetrical patterns, encouraging us to think that the symbols originally had some meaning.

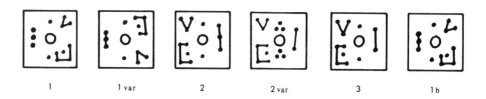

| 1 | 1 var | 2 | 2 var | 3 | 1b |

There is excellent evidence for the variety, with some 34 specimens from the Aston Rowant hoard,[33] and 15 English finds, as well as two specimens in Remmerden, one in Saint-Pierre-les-Etieux, two imitations in Bais, and a motley selection of 18 from Domburg.

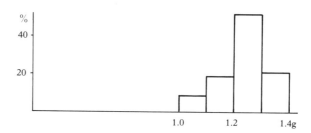

FIG. Weight pattern of Series E, VICO variety (23 specimens). See the note on the preceding text figure.

The weights of the flans are controlled with impressive accuracy, showing 70 per cent of the coins in the central step, and a modal value of c.1.25g. The four available chemical analyses record 96, 95, 95 and 94 per cent 'silver', with no measurable tin.

The large sample in the Aston Rowant hoard should give an excellent opportunity to assess the range of varieties that was available by the date of concealment, in c.705-10, and to consider whether the English single finds have the same or a more extended range, in other words whether the issue of the 'VICO' variety continued after that date.

[33] The tally includes the coins sold at Glendinings on 17 February 1988, lots 281ff., which the writer had the opportunity to weigh and photograph.

There are three sub-varieties in the hoard. The most plentiful reproduces every element of its reverse design down to the last pellet with scrupulous regularity, copied from die to die, like sacred scripture to the last jot and tittle. In particular, the symbol that has been read as a letter C is lop-sided and always has an extra pellet enclosed within its space. The letter I, so called, consists of three pellets close together in a row. Sometimes, but not always, they are joined by a line.[34] Occasionally

FIG. The **VICO** variety 1 (Aston Rowant 284b and 285a; Remmerden 76.)

the V and the C change places.[35] The resemblance to the word *Vico* is thus not impressive. On the obverse there are four parallel lines within the curve, of which the one joined to the curve is often longer, and the two furthest away are linked by a fine stroke to make an H or N. This trivial detail is again scrupulously preserved and repeated, and was evidently

FIG. The **VICO** variety 1 (Aston Rowant 285b).

understood by the die-cutter as a necessary element of the design. Beneath the four parallel lines is a triangle, usually but not always inverted.

The next sub-variety is more or less a lateral reversal of the plentiful reverse, and can more legitimately be read as **VICO**. The row of three pellets is more widely spaced, and is joined more conspicuously by a line.

FIG. The **VICO** variety 2 (Aston Rowant 286b).

[34] The examples illustrated in the text are Glendining, 17 February 1988, 284b and 285a (1.20, 1.18g).
[35] ibid., 285b (1.33g).

213

The reverse dies in particular have a different feel, and could be by another die-cutter.[36] A minor variation, known from a single find from Barham, Kent (catalogued below) introduces small groups of three pellets.

The third sub-variety could well be by the same hand as the second. Its reverse is the same, except that instead of the line with three pellets, there is a line with two pellets. The obverse is quite different: an approximate imitation of Variety G, with the two pellets superimposed on the spine of the porcupine, but lacking the group of three pellets within the curve, near the acute angle. A large annulet is inserted below the middle of the curve, which is no part of Variety G, but could perhaps echo the design of Variety D. This scarce sub-variety (about one in twenty?) is obviously official, and part of the substantive series.[37]

FIG. The **VICO** variety 3 (Aston Rowant 286c; Remmerden 146).

Although it borrows elements from the design of other Aston Rowant varieties of porcupine, it is certainly not from the workshop of Variety G, or D. The sub-variety is securely documented as being from Aston Rowant. (The specimen catalogued below may be suspected of being a stray.) It was also present in Remmerden. There is an English find from Meols, 1867,[38] and another from the Kings Lynn area find.

The English finds include clear specimens of all three sub-varieties, in roughly the same proportions as they occur in the Aston Rowant hoard. They also include another plentiful variant, like the first except that the three dots are more obviously joined by a line. It is stylistically coherent.

FIG. The **VICO** variety 1b (Royston 10).

[36] ibid., 286b (1.27g).
[37] ibid., 286c (1.28g); Remmerden 146 (1.21g); Grave-find of Unknown Provenance (1.20g, same obv.die as Remmerden?); and a coin catalogued below.
[38] *SCBI Merseyside* 20 (1.10g.)

Examples are the finds from Great Bircham,[39] Royston 9,[40] Wroot,[41] and probably Reculver XXVII.[42] If this variant (1b?) was indeed absent from Aston Rowant (and not merely from the available sample) it is presumably because it is late.

The best evidence for the relationship of Sub-varieties 1, 2, and 1b will lie in a correlation of the obverse and reverse styles. There is enough material to encourage one to expect positive results, but scarcely enough to give a definitive answer. Of the four lines within the curve, one (as already mentioned) is sometimes longer: this trait seems to be restricted to Sub-variety 1. It is accompanied on the reverse by large letters or pseudo-letters in the margin, including a reversed E.[43]

Another point of departure: a variant within Sub-variety 1 has neatly ranged, smaller letters in the margin, I I +I I Γ I I C I I, etc.[44] The V and the C have changed places, and the C has equal limbs. Some examples have a

FIG. The VICO variety 1, with pseudo-legend in reverse margin (Aston Rowant 285b).

cross in front of the porcupine, reminiscent of the same feature on the 'plumed birds'.[45] This variant was present in Aston Rowant.

In Sub-variety 2, the wider spacing of the lines within the curve, and the bolder cross-bar of the H, are a trait that is discontinuous with Sub-variety 1. The Barham find (above) is characteristic. Because of its rarity it would be natural to see it as experimental and early. Royston 10, with single pellets as normal, has the same bold H. It is rarely possible to see what is in the border of the reverse of Sub-variety 2. A couple of widely-spaced pellets are occasionally visible.

Sub-variety 1b apparently develops out of 1. The porcupine's quills perhaps tend to grow thinner and fewer, but there is not much change in style. If, as seems to be the case, there is a contrast between Aston Rowant and the English finds in the occurrence of 1b, it will indicate that the minting of the VICO variety continued a little later than the date of deposit of the hoard.

---

[39] Blackburn and Bonser, 'Single finds – 3' (note 28 above), no.94 (1.25g).

[40] ibid.

[41] 'Coin Register' 1987, no.64 (1.21g).

[42] *Sceattas in England and on the Continent,* pp.259-60.

[43] Glendining, 17 February 1988, 285a.

[44] ibid., 285b.

[45] *NC* 1966, pl.15, 4 = *BMC* 61 (1.31g).

The evidence of stylistic analysis for the **VICO** variety as a whole is that Sub-varieties 2 and 3 are probably early, 3 being imitative before the new workshop settled into its own version of the design. Whether 3-2 and 1 were concurrent is not clear. Placing the more legible sub-varieties 3-2 early has the advantage of making it more plausible that the curious, non-symmetrical design has a literal meaning. Sub-variety 1 can then be seen as a blundered and laterally reversed copy of it.

Against this view, the recent Kings Lynn find, which appears to be a little later in date than Aston Rowant, contains one specimen each of Sub-varieties 2 and 3. Both have a reversed **N** in the margin; and the former has a small cross in front of the porcupine. One may choose

FIG. The **VICO** varieties 2 and 3 (from a find in the Kings Lynn area).

between seeing these two coins as recent issues at the date of burial, or as two older coins represented in the find by chance. The very high weight of the coin of Sub-variety 2 (1.38g) may point to its being early, or again it may be a matter of chance.

The specimen in Saint-Pierre-les-Etieux, now known only from a line-drawing, appears to be of Sub-variety 1, as is the other Remmerden coin.

Those in the Bais hoard are blatant imitations – one of which manages to copy the leg and claws of the plumed bird.

From Bawsey there is a counterfeit double-reverse coin which combines the cross-and-pellets of Series D with a (Sub-variety 1?) **VICO** reverse.

IV

The ubiquitous Variety G has been intensively studied by Blackburn and Bonser, who propose a sub-division into G1, G2, G3, and G4. The weights of the flans are impressively exactly adjusted, and it is very clear that G4 is on a lower standard than G1-3. Of the former, 70 per cent of the weights fall in a single step, and there is a modal value of $c.1.25$g for coins from a mixture of sources. The Aston Rowant hoard suggests a figure of 1.26 or 1.27g. G4 falls to $c.1.05$g.

The alloy is consistently $c.94$-95 per cent 'silver'. The one specimen of

FIG. Series E, Varieties G1-4. (After Blackburn and Bonser, *BNJ* 57 (1987), 99-103.)

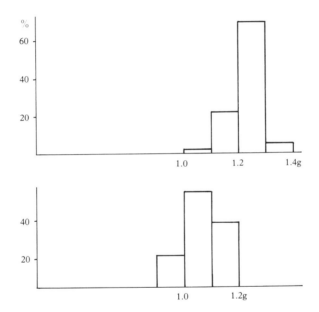

FIG. Weight patterns of Series E, Variety G. Top: Varieties G1-3 (40 specmens). Bottom: Variety G4 (6 specimens). See the note on the 'plumed bird' varieties.

G4 that has been analysed showed 94 per cent. The coins are tin-free, but contain the usual trifling amounts of zinc.

G1 is recognizably in finer style than G2-3. The group of three pellets near the acute angle is small and neat. Beneath the porcupine there is a distinctive rectangular box enclosing an **X**. In one margin of the reverse is an equally distinctive reversed **И**, possibly reminiscent of the tufa on the prototype, but here clearly treated as a letter, with pellet serifs.

217

A rare variant of G1 has, on the reverse, added groups of three pellets, creating the same formal pattern as Variety J of the 'plumed birds'. There seems to be a cross in one margin, again as seen on the 'plumed birds'. This coin (catalogued below) could be a genuine G1/J mule, but the workmanship of the reverse die is nearer to G1. Perhaps it is an early, experimental version – G0.

FIG. Variety G, with 3 added pellets (G0).

G2 is coarser. The rectangular box is either off the flan or perhaps has disappeared from the design. A specimen with an almost empty standard on the reverse (containing only the central annulet and pellet), Blackburn and Bonser 15,[46] may be an accidentally unfinished die.

G3 lacks the group of three pellets near the acute angle. Beneath the porcupine one can often see traces of a zig-zag line, at the very edge of the flan. There is at least one badly centred specimen from Aston Rowant[47] which shows that it is the Z of the legend referred to below, as found on G4. Other off-centre specimens allow us to see some of the motifs used in the reverse border, which include a bar with three pellets.[48]

A specimen assigned to G3, from the Saint-Pierre-les-Etieux hoard[49] has a cross in one reverse margin, but the obverse style is erratic, and the coin may well be an imitation.

In G4 the two pellets superimposed on the curve of the porcupine are transferred more or less to the space beneath it. Beneath the porcupine is the distinctive legend or pseudo-legend XAZO, the final O being diamond-shaped and inserted into the bend of the Z.[50] The reversed И of the reverse margin is a regular feature of G4, although it is sketchily drawn and unseriffed.

The Aston Rowant hoard contained at least 2 specimens of G1, at least 4 of G2, and at least 11 of G3, but none of G4. It provides reasonably clear evidence that the issue of G4 post-dates the hoard.

The age-structure of this group of specimens of Variety G appears to be normal (but we do not know the relative scale of issue of G1, 2, and 3). Blackburn and Bonser explore the idea that G1 might be from a different mint.[51] We have seen (above) that great quantities of evidence from the

---

[46] Glendining, 283b (1.33g).
[47] ibid., 283c.
[48] Glendining, 13 March 1975, 238 and 240.

[49] Blackburn and Bonser 17 = Saint-Pierre-les Etieux 97.
[50] ibid., 25.   [51] ibid., at pp.101-2.

Rhine mouths area would be needed to prove that the early porcupines came from more than one mint there. In this particular case, there is, apart from the difference of style which can be interpreted as early, no other reason to multiply mints.

In the Remmerden hoard there were three specimens of G3. In Saint-Pierre-les-Etieux there were one of G2 and two of G3. No.76 in that hoard, now known only from a line-drawing, is ostensibly a 'mule' of G3 with a coin of Marseilles. Its obverse is so similar to that of no.97 that one wonders whether two unrelated drawings have not been inadvertently paired – a suspicion confirmed by the double-reverse coin, no.99, again known only from a line-drawing, which can be seen to include the reverse of no.97f. In the Nohanent hoard there are two specimens apparently of G2. Bais had a G2 and a G3. In Cimiez there was a G1.

Imitations of Variety G include a find from Caistor-by-Norwich with lateral reversal (catalogued below). It is 94 per cent 'silver', but weighs only 0.90g. Another imitation, of better weight, is again 94 per cent fine; the four bars in the standard have been rearranged into a rotating pattern.[52] Bais 309d (1.10g) is closely similar and obviously from the same stable.

A copy of G4 (below) has a reverse which owes something to the VICO variety.

V

A little care is needed in identifying Variety D, as there are secondary porcupines with a formally similar reverse design. The variety as defined by the dozen specimens present in the Aston Rowant hoard[53] has a

FIG. Variety D (Aston Rowant 281 a and b).

distinctive porcupine obverse, with a small triangle at one end of the curve, and a bold annulet at the other end – usually but not always attached to the curve. Beneath are two pellets, which can be fine or

---

[52] Catalogued below.

[53] *Coin Hoards* 1 gives the total as 10, to which may be added Glendining, 17 February 1988, 281a and b (1.27, 1.24g). Three specimens catalogued below are from Sotheby, 17 July 1986, 186. There were two specimens in Sotheby, 18 July 1985, 502, of which one was illustrated.

coarse, and a large cross pommee. There is normally a fine pellet within the triangle. The workmanship is untidy and variable, but the elements of the design are consistent.

The square of the standard on the reverse is relatively small, and the workmanship is again rough. The square contains the very simple pattern of a central annulet (normally pelletted) and four pellets cross-wise. The broad margin generally has a legend or pseudo-legend, which seems to include the letters QV or OV, and sometimes an elongated square ⊏. The letter-form Q is reminiscent of the mint-signature for Quentovic on early Carolingian coins, of Pepin and Charlemagne. That (slender) parallel, and finds from Ardres (a few miles south-east of Calais, a region not rich in sceatta finds), from Dorchester, Dorset, and from Ogbourne St. Andrew, Wilts. have prompted the suggestion that Variety D might be from Quentovic.[54] There is a stylistically related (secondary?) porcupine from Hanford, Dorset.

Fig. Variety D (Ogbourne St. Andrew find).

The broader view will take account, however, of finds in the same style from Caistor-by-Norwich,[55] Claxby (Lincs.),[56] near Grimsby,[57] and Whitby[58] – a classically east-coast distribution. There is also an imitation from Bawsey, Norfolk.[59]

A sample of weights of Aston Rowant specimens (1.29, 1.27, 1.24, 1.20, 1.16g.) shows no difference from the other three early varieties. The heaviest of the five coins contains 96 per cent 'silver', and the two lightest 88 and 94 per cent respectively, with traces of tin.

Among the English single finds, lighter weights prevail (1.15, 1.13, 1.00, 0.96g). The discrepancy will be partly the usual small difference between hoard coins and stray finds. There may also have been a decline or reduction in average weight. The roughness and variability of the design make it impossible, without more material, to correlate style and metrology at all confidently. Variety D may have continued in issue after the date of deposit of Aston Rowant, as Varieties G and 'VICO' seem to have done.

---

[54] Metcalf, in *Wilts Arch.Mag.* (note 5 above). (1.15g).

[55] Christies, 4 November 1986, lot 359.

[56] Blackburn and Bonser, 'Single finds – 1', no.4

[57] ibid., no.9 (1.00g).

[58] *NC* 1966, pl.16, 30 (1.13g).

[59] Catalogued below.

VI

The exact mint-place or places of the early porcupines is an enigma. There are no significant contrasts of metrology or distribution between them, but it remains puzzling that four such different designs should have been minted concurrently at Dorestad. New evidence, e.g. from the excavation of Quentovic, might change our view.

The only other possiblity is that evidence from the next phase of the porcupines might throw some retrospective light on the problem.

SERIES E: THE LATER PORCUPINES

THE VAST trackless wastes of the later porcupines can be mapped only sketchily. In sharpest contrast with the four substantive varieties of the Aston Rowant phase, each clearly defined, there is a medley of carelessly executed designs, with few if any hard and fast categories. The characteristic TOT/II design makes its appearance, often with extra pellets or groups of pellets between the letters. It is usually, but not always, associated with an obverse having three or four parallel lines within the curve. Obverses with a triangular snout are also plentiful. They usually have a cross pommee and an annulet beneath the curve, like the earlier Variety D, but not in any precise or fixed place in relation to the curve. The associated reverses tend to be diagonally symmetrical, sometimes with a 'mixed grill' of symbols, L X L C around the central annulet. Other obverses have XII or XIII within the curve. Others are quite eccentric. But one cannot divide the coins up into categories without being confronted by numerous exceptions which do not conform to the criteria. And the scale of the problem is massive. Anyone who has had the task of searching for comparanda for a newly-discovered porcupine will know that there is a seemingly endless range of variation. Many hundreds of dies were used. Differences in the pattern of the outer border of the reverse are a reminder that there were no doubt a number of die-cutters. It would be natural, too, given the scale of the issues, that there should have been many moneyers. Disturbingly, obverse die-links show that quite different reverse types were sometimes produced concurrently in the same workshop. The porcupines were cleverly counterfeited, the characteristic TOT/II reverse design being 'muled', for example, in the English Series R. Such coins are easily recognized, but there may well have been even more which imitated both obverse and reverse, and passed as genuine porcupines. The workmanship of the official dies is frequently so slap-dash and untidy, that it is difficult to draw the line between regular coins and copies, unless the latter are plated or seriously debased. All in all, the problem of describing the later porcupines in ways that correspond with the arrangements for their minting is daunting.

Searching for die-links will help to establish some hard facts, but it will not carry the student very far towards an over-view of what was, probably, the most plentiful of all sceatta coinages. It is not just that we have so far failed to grasp the pattern implicit in the many variations of design: to a significant extent, it seems that there was no pattern. Any idea that one could, by prolonged effort, resolve the detailed information into a tidy scheme of classification is almost certainly illusory. Collectors might be pleased, and satisfied, to be provided with charts of variant designs against which to match the specimens in their collections, but unless one can demonstrate the order in which the coins were produced – the 'where' and 'when' for each variety – one has not classified, but merely listed them.

If the typology is confused, it follows that the appropriate strategy is first to concentrate on getting the broad perspectives drawn more or less correctly, by distancing oneself from the detail, and by taking full account of aspects of the porcupines that are independent of their stylistic variation, in particular their weight and alloy.

From these it will appear that the chaos implied by the stylistic variation is more apparent than real. Nevertheless, with the beginning of the secondary phase the porcupines undergo a sea-change. From being a straight-forward, well-ordered fourfold series of issues of impeccable primary quality, they seem suddenly to break off or to change the character of their die-cutting, becoming extremely variable. Their average weight, however, remains very high – unusually so for secondary sceattas. The modal value is the same as in the primary phase. The spread of weights changes, becoming wide. The alloy sinks to 80-85 per cent silver, or sometimes even less. What happened? One thinks of the analogy of the later Northumbrian stycas, another profuse and intractable series, which also suffered a sea-change, becoming imitative and meaningless in their legends. Earlier issues of stycas were copied at random, sometimes crudely but often quite well. Extensive chains of die-linking (the stycas have had a very high survival-rate) show that the moneyers' names can no longer be assumed to be an indication of the officials responsible for the quality of the coins. The die-cutters blatantly produced meaningless dies.[1] One cannot truthfully claim that the radical changes in the organization of the York coinage could have been foreseen or predicted from what little we know about the political history of Northumbria in the relevant decades. The exact dating of the stycas is, unfortunately, contentious and has proved difficult to establish, in

[1] E. J. E. Pirie, 'Phases and groups within the styca coinage of Northumbria', in D. M. Metcalf (editor), *Coinage in Ninth-Century Northumbria*, Oxford, 1987, pp.103-145.

relation to the capture of York by the Vikings. The imitative coins seem to belong to a phase of political weakness and strife within the Northumbrian kingdom, some time before the capture of York – an internal weakness, perhaps, which exposed the kingdom to the threat of external attack.[2] In saying that the coins belong to that phase, we are in effect constructing a plausible hypothesis linking the organizational aspects of the coinage with the general historical background, – with the benefit of hindsight, so to speak. Equally we may invent an explanantion for the confused designs of the later porcupines by trying out a similar hypothesis (although it begs many questions), linking the confusion of minting in Dorestad with political changes in greater Frisia. The struggle between Pepin and the Frisian king Redbad is known to us through the life of St. Willibrord. We learn that after Pepin's death the balance of power shifted in Redbad's favour. In 716 he penetrated up the Rhine as far as Köln with his fleet, and defeated Charles Martel there. Utrecht fell into Frisian hands. In the same year Boniface took ship from London to Dorestad, where he found a tense situation. He travelled to Utrecht to meet Redbad, but the meeting was fruitless and he returned to England. In 719 Redbad died and Charles Martel resumed the offensive against Frisia, which he conquered as far as the mouth of the Rhine. In 734 he defeated the Frisian fleet and pushed the Merovingian frontier to the River Lauwers, the boundary between the modern provinces of Friesland and Groningen.[3]

The year 716 lies close to the date at which the secondary phase of porcupines began, so far as we can judge. The Aston Rowant hoard was deposited c.705-10, and a comparison between the hoard and the English site-finds has shown that the early phase of four distinct varieties continued for a few years longer. Thus the post-Aston Rowant porcupines, which must have been issued over a couple of decades if not longer, will certainly find their political context in the struggle for power between the Merovingian and Frisian rulers. Dorestad was a major prize in that struggle, and it lay uncomfortably close to the zone of conflict – and on the Frisian side of the Rhine distributaries. We can postulate cause and effect, by putting forward the hypothesis that the disorganized appearance of the sceattas reflects the local impact, at Dorestad, of the political uncertainties in the Rhine mouths area. It is a rather general hypothesis, and will only acquire merit if ways can be found of testing it.

[2] H. E. Pagan, 'Northumbrian numismatic chronology in the ninth century', *BNJ* 38 (1969), 1-15; D. P. Kirby, 'Northumbria in the ninth century', in *CNCN*, pp.11-25.

[3] P. C. J. A. Boeles, *Friesland tot de elfde eeuw. Zijn vóór- en vroege geschiedenis*, The Hague, 1951, pp.269-87 (and 585f.). Boeles's chronology for the coinage is now, alas, out of date.

224

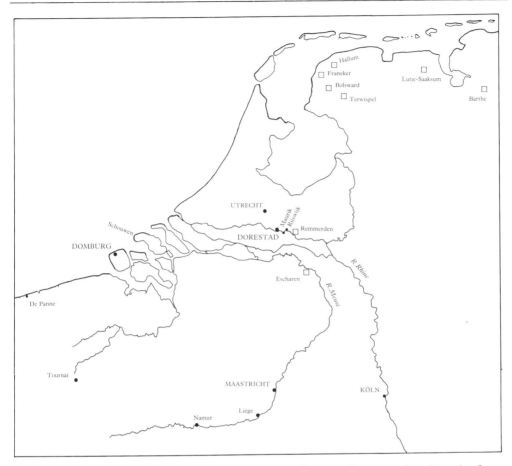

MAP. The Rhine mouths area, the Meuse valley, and porcupine hoards from Friesland.

One can think of alternative hypotheses, for example that some of the porcupines were minted by the Frisians elsewhere than at Dorestad, presumably further to the north, in territory ruled by Redbad or his successors, in imitation of the commercially known and trusted Merovingian issues. It is what the Vikings did in the English Danelaw, and one can think of other examples of such upstart behaviour. If it were the case, how (we should ask ourselves) could one distinguish the two categories of coinage for purposes of classification? – It comes down to simple questions of fact: when and where the later porcupines were struck. Unless we can demonstrate detailed answers to the two constant questions, we are in a cloud-cuckoo-land of happy speculation.

225

The chronology of the sceattas is for the most part a relative chronology, anchored to absolute dates only here and there – and even then, only arguably so. The dating of the Aston Rowant hoard seems secure enough, but it is anchored only at one remove to dates in the history of Marseilles, with a latitude of five or more years. The persistence of the four primary varieties of porcupines for a short time post Aston Rowant again seems secure enough, but it is a matter of guesswork how long minting continued. We are fortunate, therefore, to have some completely independent evidence. Against the dates of events in the struggle between Charles Martel and Redbad we may set the latest archaeological evidence from Ribe, in Jutland, which is so specific that the dates it provides are tantamount to absolute dates.

The excavations on the post office site at Ribe in 1990 were undertaken after the astonishing implications of the coins from the 1970-6 excavations had been thoroughly digested. The potential interest of a secure chronology was well understood before work began. The techniques of excavation were therefore as up-to-date and as scrupulous as care could make them. The stratigraphy of the site, as it turned out, was wonderfully clear and detailed. Sceattas began to be plentiful in layer C, which was securely dated by dendrochronology to the 720s. With dendrochronology there are of course no margins of statistical imprecision, such as attend C^{14} dating. Care was taken to use samples of wood which were lying horizontally in layer C, not vertical posts which might have become displaced. The earliest losses of sceattas on the site came from the underlying layers B2 and B3. The excavators were entirely confident that layer B2 antedated C (even if the finds from the sloping layer B3, near its boundary with C, were liable to incorrect interpretation). The assemblage of half-a-dozen sceattas from B2 was late-primary in flavour, but it already included one secondary porcupine. The coin seems to be imitative (i.e. possibly local) but it clearly copies the plentiful TOT / II variety with a group of three dots added between the symbols I, I – which it must post-date. A date of loss for this coin a little earlier than c.720 is indicated. The introduction of the Frisian prototype will not necessarily have been more than a year or so earlier than the striking of the copy, on the tightest possible chronological scheme. The gap may have been greater. The evidence from Ribe, therefore, again points towards a date of origin for the secondary porcupines close to 716, if not earlier – but in any case hardly later.

I

There are several hoards containing porcupines, each of which should provide a *terminus ante quem* for the varieties it included. In the same way that we can speak of an Aston Rowant phase, referring to the porcupines minted essentially in the ten or fifteen years up to the date of deposit of that hoard, so we ought to be able to use two important later hoards (which will be discussed below) to define a Kloster Barthe phase and a Franeker phase, and thus to carry our exploration of the porcupines forward by stages, from A to B, from B to C, and from C to D. Whether or not the later porcupines include Frisian imitations, their date of issue should be an unambiguous matter of fact: any varieties, or dies, represented in a hoard will most certainly be earlier than the deposit of the hoard. And we are fortunate in having abundant evidence by which to define the phases. The Kloster Barthe hoard of 1838, from the region of Leer in Ostfriesland, was a very large hoard of at least 780 porcupines, together with one specimen of the 'stepped cross' variety. Of these, 752 coins, in splendid condition, are preserved in the Emden Museum.[4] Secondly, the Franeker hoard, from near Leeuwarden, contained about 360 porcupines, of which 189 were described, with illustrations, by Dirks.[5] Various smaller hoards add another couple of hundred coins. There are in addition some 400 single finds of later porcupines from Domburg, and a hundred or so single finds from England.

In spite of this wealth of material, the difficulty remains that the hoards do not enable us to construct a classification of the later porcupines according to their chronology, except in the broadest terms. The distinctive coins which make up the Franeker hoard are quite separate and are no doubt late; outside the hoard, they are not plentiful. Otherwise, the whole problem lies within the second stage, from B to C. The Kloster Barthe hoard contains, apparently, the full stylistic range and endless variety of secondary porcupines with which we have to come to terms.

There are some other, smaller hoards of similar coins which might, in

[4] See *SCBI Berlin*, p.12. The coins at Emden, studied and arranged by Professor P. Berghaus, have been photographed, enlarged x 2½, by Dr. David Hill, to whom I am indebted for a photocopy of his record of the hoard, including weights.

[5] The hoard is discussed and a selection of coins illustrated in J. Dirks, *Les Anglo-Saxons et leurs petits deniers dits sceattas*, Brussels, 1870, at pp.58f. and pp.70f., note 4. It seems that these coins are now in the Royal Coin Collection. A die-study of them should be possible.

principle, provide us with an independent standpoint from which to take a critical view of Kloster Barthe. They might be a little earlier or later; or they might, conceivably, have a different regional flavour. Unfortunately they are numerically too small to allow us to establish a contrast with Kloster Barthe, given the complexity of the series. They may one day come into their own, if the chemical compositions of the coins can be accurately measured. Two of the hoards remain unpublished.

The Lutje Saaksum hoard of 27 porcupines, from an east Frisian find-spot towards Jever, has been published with full illustration.[6] So has a parcel of 35 coins which came into the hands of the firm of Franceschi.[7] The speculation has been profferred that they are another part of the Lutje Saaksum hoard. It is perhaps just as likely that they are half the vanished Stephanik hoard, found before 1904 somewhere in the province of Friesland. Of the 78 sceattas it is known to have contained, 72 were porcupines.[8] The Föhr hoard, from an island off the west coast of Jutland, consists of 77 sceattas, of which 56 are porcupines. The hoard is dated by a denier from the middle of the century, naming Milo. Its publication is awaited.[9] All these hoards, and those of Kloster Barthe, Franeker, and Hallum (described below), lie far beyond the area of the Rhine mouths, in the coasts of Frisia and towards the Northern Lands. They are a reminder of the trade-route, or one of the trade-routes, on which Dorestad's prosperity rested.

There is just one tiny hoard from Wijk-bij-Duurstede itself. It was found in 1846 and is unpublished, but reportedly contained two of the same (late) varieties as were present in Franeker.[10] That hoard, as already mentioned, is made up of a completely different currency of porcupines, struck on distinctly larger flans, and falling into just three substantive varieties in an orderly way. One of the three is very clearly affiliated to the VICO variety. That being so, we may accept that a second variety is affiliated to Variety G of the early porcupines. The third variety has no obvious antecedents. The Franeker hoard also includes two or three specimens of smaller, nondescript porcupines, which would not (in our present state of information) look out of place in the Kloster Barthe hoard. Perhaps they are strays, surviving from the earlier issues. There

[6] P. V. Hill, 'Two hoard of sceattas from the Province of Groningen', *JMP* 42 (1955), 104-5, and pl.10; D. Hill and J. Sharples, 'The Lutje Saaksum hoard: a correction', ibid., 60-1 (1973-4), 156-8.

[7] D. M. Metcalf, 'A hoard of "porcupine" sceattas', *American Numismatic Society Museum Notes* 15 (1969), 101-18.

[8] W. Op den Velde, W. J. de Boone, and A. Pol, '

A survey of sceatta finds from the Netherlands', in *Sceattas in England and on the Continent*, pp.117-45, at p.143, s.v. Unknown Provenance.

[9] K. Bendixen, 'Finds of sceattas from Scandinavia', ibid., pp.151-7, at p.152.

[10] Op den Velde et al., loc.cit., at p. 142 (six coins of Varieties E and F).

are, conversely, no Franeker-type strays in Kloster Barthe.

Is it possible, however, that we have two contemporary regional currencies, and that Franeker, rather than being late, is merely a sum of money that was close to its source, in the sense of having been kept intact since it left the mint? Might that not make sense of the continuity from Varieties G and VICO? The implication would be that the Kloster Barthe coins were Frisian while the Franeker coins were Merovingian – without prejudice to the question where each was struck. Given the uncertainties of the political context, that question should be left open. We should expect the numismatic context, also, to be blurred. If Kloster Barthe varieties had been minted beyond the Rhine distributaries, they would still doubtless have circulated in large quantities at Dorestad and Domburg. We can only guess at the proportions. The statistics from the major sites will therefore in principle not tell us unequivocally about the region of origin of the two kinds of porcupines.

There are enough Franeker-type single finds at Middelburg with a probable Domburg provenance to represent the losses of a period in which they circulated there, and they include the same range of varieties in much the same proportions as the hoard. Coins from the Marie de Man collection are probably also mostly from Domburg, but we do not know how far she may have acquired coins from elsewhere. Many of the porcupines in the Koninklijk Penningkabinet unfortunately became separated from their tickets, and therefore their provenances, fifty years ago. The residue of the non-hoard specimens of Franeker type can now only be reconstructed from the evidence of patination. The occurrence of the Franeker varieties in the Low Countries is, in a word, known only rather vaguely.

The English evidence comes to the rescue. The extreme scarcity of Franeker varieties among the English single finds absolutely precludes their having been contemporary with the Kloster Barthe varieties which are, if not exactly plentiful, at least moderately common in England. Whatever political constraints may from time to time have been imposed on free trade across the North Sea, the virtual absence of Franeker varieties in England can only be because they are late in date.

Our conclusion therefore is that the workmen who produced the three substantive varieties which make up the Franeker phase were reverting to obsolete designs, after a lapse of time. Perhaps, on the historical hypothesis with which we began, it happened fairly soon after Charles Martel's victory in 734. The alternative view has been canvassed that the Franeker hoard is still later, from a date much closer to the reform of

Pepin – or even that it is contemporary with the early Carolingian coinage. The large numbers of single finds of early Carolingian coins from Wijk-bij-Duurstede and from the Rhine mouths area generally make the latter view seem unlikely. The difficulty of ruling it out altogether, however, underlines the vagueness of the absolute chronology.

The relative chronology is, in the end, uncontroversial. The Kloster Barthe phase is the middle phase. With over 750 coins available for study, it ought to be a superb source from which to delineate the issues of porcupines from the years preceding its deposit. But we cannot hope to use the hoard for purposes of stylistic analysis in the normal way, because we cannot trust the designs of the coins to make sense. Unless a substantial hoard concealed eight or ten years earlier becomes available, our best hope of progress lies in finding some other way of analysing its age-structure.

There are, it is true, three hoards which seem to be intermediate in date between Aston Rowant and Kloster Barthe, but they contain the merest handful of secondary porcupines. They are the recent find of 20 coins from the Kings Lynn area, probably a grave-find, the Hallum hoard, and the Cimiez hoard.

The conjectural grave-find included 4 porcupines alongside various primary sceattas.[11] Its age-structure looks very compact, and it seems to belong only a few years later than Aston Rowant – at most five years. Subject only to the proviso that the coins were not recovered by archaeologists in controlled circumstances, the early dating is exceptionally secure. Three of the porcupines are of Aston Rowant varieties (VICO, 2; G, 1), but the fourth is quite unrelated and, one would have said, of

poorer than average secondary quality. A closely similar coin, discussed below, is of poor alloy. The natural interpretataion is that neither of them was minted in the workshops of the primary porcupines. They are probably imitations, although not exactly meant to deceive, since the pattern in the reverse standard is distinctive. The English find weighs only 1.01g, and the comparandum 1.10g. It may be, then, that there is

[11] I am indebted to the free-lance cleaner, who lent me plaster casts of the hoard and discussed his observations on the patina of the coins before cleaning.

more than one strand among the secondary porcupines, and that from the very beginning of the secondary phase, we must be prepared to find imitations.

The Hallum hoard of 1866, from the north Frisian coast, contained at least 223 sceattas predominantly of Series X, the exact dating of which remains debateable. There were 13 porcupines, and a few English coins which point towards an early secondary date.[12] The crucial coins are

FIG. Later porcupines in the Hallum hoard. (After Dirks. Top row: Dirks, pl.C, 7, 8, 9, 3, 2, 11. Bottom row: pl.C, 1, 10, 5, 6, 4.)

two[13] of Series J, Type 85 (BIIIb) and an early coin of Series Q (Dirks, pl.D, 31). These establish a *terminus post quem*, which is supported by three quite early-looking specimens of Series G.[14] The association of G and J is reminiscent of the Garton-on-the-Wolds grave-find. Judging the date of concealment on the evidence, essentially, of three strays which were foreign coins and which made up less than 2 per cent of the total is not particularly secure, the more so as there was an imitative coin in the hoard which seems to be derivative from the two standing figures type of Series N or, more probably, of Type 30.[15] There was also a scarce LVNDONIA 5/12 mule, which would point towards an even later date, if it is derivative from Series L, Type 12. Philip Hill stated categorically,

[12] Dirks, op.cit., p.56 and note 2, with Plates C1 – D31.

[13] Or one?

[14] Pl.D, 19-21.

[15] Pl.C, 13.

however, that it was not part of the Hallum hoard.[16]

A dating based on the English evidence raises questions about the English chronology, rather than providing answers applicable to the continental hoards. If the two standing figures type is indeed derived from Series N or from Type 30, rather than from some non-numismatic repertoire of motifs, it hints at a surprisingly early date for the introduction of the English types. The specimens of Series G and J in Hallum suggest a t.p.q. of 'Aston Rowant plus *c.* ten years'. If we stretch that to fifteen, to allow for the two standing figures type, it probably carries us about ten years into the secondary phase of the porcupines. That is presumably still somewhat earlier than the date of the Kloster Barthe hoard, but it is frankly a matter of guesswork to say how many years separate Hallum and Kloster Barthe.

The 13 porcupines already include a range of reverse designs, which seems to be as variable (so far as the sample size allows us to say) as that found in the Kloster Barthe hoard. It is not possible to establish a contrast which could then be used to divide the Kloster Barthe coins, even very roughly, into pre- and post-Hallum phases. The 13 include two 'plumed bird' porcupines, surviving from the primary phase. There are few such coins in Kloster Barthe,[17] and certainly not two-thirteenths of the total, which would be 116 coins. That could be either because Hallum is significantly earlier in date, or because it is more miscellaneous in character, with a less tidy age-structure. One should not build too much on a couple of coins which are perhaps just strays in the hoard.

The third hoard, Cimiez, is dated to *c.*720. Le Gentilhomme illustrates 21 porcupines from it, of which 9 are primary varieties, or close copies of them. The remaining 12 coins are secondary.[18] That ratio of primary to secondary coins may be because Cimiez is earlier than Hallum, or again it may be (more plausibly) because Cimiez has a more extended age-structure and is generally more bizarre. There is the added complication that one cannot be completely sure that all Morel-Fatio's sceattas came from the hoard. The evidence of Cimiez as to which varieties of secondary porcupines are early will become stronger when it can be confirmed from the independent information of another hoard. Meanwhile, we can compare the spread of weights among the Cimiez coins with the spread in, say, Kloster Barthe: the difference (see below)

[16] Pl.C, 14. I am indebted to Professor H. B. Mattingly who arranged for Dr. P. V. Hill's plaster casts to come to the Ashmolean.

[17] In Dr. D. H. Hill's photos, ELM 378 and 641 are of the VICO variety, and 368 and probably 430

are Variety D. These are labelled 7502/14-I-4, 7503/5-V-1, 7502/13-IV-7, and 7502/15-IV-1.

[18] P. le Gentilhomme, 'La circulation des sceattas dans la Gaule mérovingienne', *RN*[5] 2 (1938), 23-49.

certainly places a question-mark against Cimiez as a guide to classification of the porcupines.

Imitations could, of course, have begun even during the primary
phase. Lafaurie has published two coins as being from the Bais hoard,
from the former collection of Louis Durocher, rediscovered by his
grandson.[19] Without being unduly sceptical, one is entitled to reserve
judgement on the evidence of two coins, to which a false provenance may
have become attached.

The standard numismatic procedure of analysing a sequence of hoards
in order to show the order in which successive varieties entered the
currency does little to clarify the later porcupines. The earlier hoards, in
particular Hallum, suggest that most if not all of the formal variants were
present from an early date. Cimiez points to the early prevalence of
copying. Die-linkage shows that different reverse designs were muled
together, thus suggesting that the types were no longer being used as a
means of exercising supervision over the moneyers. The scale of the
problem is such that finding die-links will not go far towards elucidating
it. A systematic search for die-duplication will give a rough idea of the
scale of the currency (which was prodigious), and will show what the
normal obverse:reverse die-ratio was. Die-duplication should also help us
to assess the character of the larger hoards. That is about as much as one
can hope for.

In order to move forward, we need the input of a further, independent
category of information, which can be tested for correlation with what
has been assembled so far. A thorough study of metrology offers the best
prospect. Alterations in the weight-standard, or in the accuracy with
which the flans were adjusted, should be a good indicator that batches of
coin were produced separately – although it may not be obvious whether
they point to a difference of date or place. The same is true of alterations
in the average silver contents.

II

The weights of over seven hundred porcupines in the Kloster Barthe
hoard vary very widely, from 0.82g to 1.58g. They generate a histogram
which, nevertheless, has a normal profile with a single peak, and a quite
respectable proportion of 41 per cent of the values in the central step.

[19] M. Prou and E. Bougenot, *Catalogue des deniers
mérovingiens de la trouvaille de Bais (Ille-et-Vilaine)*,
edited by J. Lafaurie, nos.309A and B.

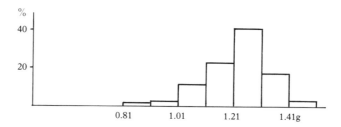

FIG. Weight pattern of Series E, later varieties (750 specimens in the Kloster Barthe hoard). See the note on the 'plumed bird' varieties.

The modal value is *c*.1.25g, which is virtually identical with that for the early porcupines, even if the proportion of coins in the central step is not as high.

Such a spreading histogram as that for the Kloster Barthe hoard as a whole, with considerable negative skewness, could easily be concealing small groups of coins which on their own would generate different patterns. There are, for example, 17 coins in the hoard with a reverse design of four pellets around an annulet; some of them have a double square border. Most but not all of them are stylistically related.[20] Their histogram has 76 per cent of the values in the central step. Even allowing

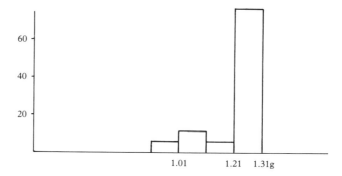

FIG. Weight pattern within the Kloster Barthe hoard: coins with rev., four pellets around central annulet (17 specimens).

for some incorrect grouping, and for the smallness of the sample, it is clear that the workmen were operating to stricter standards. The 17 coins include three pairs of duplicates.[21]

[20] Nos. 37-8, 42-3, 108, 179, 206, 327-8, 379, 408, 413, 478, 481, 483, 613, 639.

[21] Nos. 37-8, 42-3, and 327-8. For what it is worth, that implies a total of roughly 40 dies.

The large number of specimens in the hoard allows one to explore the metrology by provisionally grouping the more plentiful variant designs, in order to see whether they differ significantly from the over-all pattern. The procedure is a rough and ready one, because one cannot be sure how the coins should be grouped. No differences emerge clearly, except in one further case.

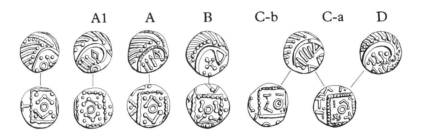

FIG. Varieties from the Kloster Barthe hoard which are involved in multiple die-duplication. ELM 410 (1 specimen), 736 (die A1, 1 specimen), 676-93 (die A, 18 specimens), 648-75 (die B, 28 specimens), 715-34 (dies C-b, 20 specimens), 702-14 (dies C-a, 13 specimens), and 739-40 (dies D-a, linked to C-a, 2 specimens).

Three obverse dies[22] are each represented in the hoard by a large number of duplicates – 18, 28, and 33. There are plenty of pairs of die-linked coins in the hoard, and a few triplets and quadruplets. These multiple die-identities, however, are statistically discontinuous with the rest of the hoard.[23] The presumption will be that they have stayed

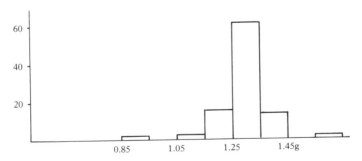

FIG. Weight pattern within the Kloster Barthe hoard: multiple die-identities and associated coins (close in date to the concealment of the hoard?). (82 specimens).

[22] Another pair of dies, very similar to the first, which is eccentric and very unusual in its designs, is represented by only one specimen; and another obverse die, represented by only two specimens, is linked to C-a (see diagram).

[23] i.e. there are no groups of 5-10 duplicates.

together since leaving the mint. They are therefore likely to be among the most recent coins in the hoard, although that is not necessarily the case. The 82 coins in question are somewhat heavier, and distinctly better adjusted, than the coins in the hoard as a whole.

Two die-identical specimens of the combination C-a were illustrated in the Stephanik sale catalogue. They raise the question, which must however remain unanswered, whether the Stephanik hoard was a parcel from Kloster Barthe. If the dies were heavily used, they might of course be represented by more than one specimen in a different hoard. The pattern of dies A and A1 occurs in the Lutje Saaksum hoard (pl.10, 9), where the coin in question may, if it is late, be useful in dating the hoard. There is also an English single find of the same variety, catalogued below.

The Franceschi parcel yields a histogram which is indistinguishable from that for Kloster Barthe, so far as can be expected from a sample of only 35 coins.

The Cimiez coins, mentioned above, are lighter and less regular.

Dirks published a selection of weights for the Franeker coins which he

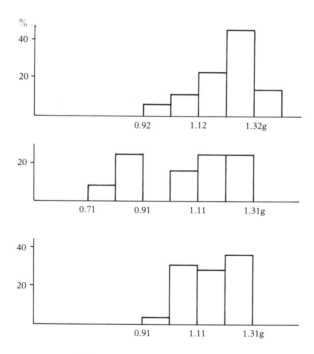

FIG. Weight patterns of later porcupines. Top: the Franceschi parcel (35 specimens). Middle: the Cimiez hoard (12 specimens). Bottom: the Franeker coins (Dirks's sample).

236

illustrated. They should serve provisionally to give an idea of the weight-standard of the late porcupines. They are lighter, and well-controlled. The average weight of *c*.1.17g points, again, towards a reform.

As regards the Kloster Barthe phase, there is no evidence of a decline in weight, nor can one point to any differences within the sample which might help to classify it, except for the group of unusually heavy die-duplicates. It is possible that their weight compensates for a reduction in fineness, but we have no evidence on that point, except that an English find from closely related dies (the Woodmansey find, catalogued below) is only 64% silver.

III

Eight specimens from the Franceschi parcel have been chemically analysed by EPMA,[24] and two more by XRF spectrometry. Duplicate analyses show that other earlier XRF results were usually a little too high, because of surface enrichment. A histogram of the finenesses shows that they cluster around 80-85 per cent 'silver'. A specimen which is only

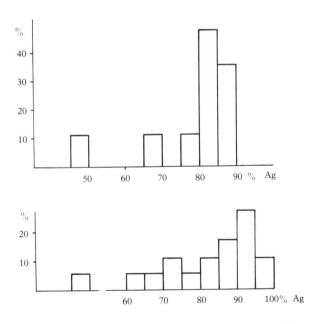

FIG. 'Silver' contents of later porcupines. Top: coins in the Franceschi parcel (8 specimens). Bottom: other coins in the Ashmolean Museum (18 specimens).

[24] By Dr. J. P. Northover.

237

67 per cent silver is stylistically very close to the coin (above) in the recent English grave-find. As for the coin with only 46 per cent silver, it is easy to believe from its style that it is an unofficial product.

Comparable EPMA results for other specimens in the Ashmolean collection show a wider spread, and in particular many results of over 90 per cent silver. There is no immediately obvious correlation between the basic designs and the finenesses.

The evidence as a whole suggests that there was an earlier phase, perhaps no longer well represented in the Franceschi parcel, and that the average silver contents declined during the secondary phase. The English evidence may exaggerate the early secondary phase: we have seen that there was a sharp decline in numbers between the primary and secondary porcupines relative to their occurrence on the Continent. A fuller programme of EPMA investigations will be needed to test this view. It could usefully be based on a comparison between the Hallum and Kloster Barthe hoards. In the latter there are enough pairs and triplets of die-duplicates to establish the tolerated variability of the alloy.

Meanwhile, a correlation of silver and tin contents tends to support the hypothesis of a declining standard. Coins with less than 75 per cent silver have over 1.5 per cent tin added.

IV

Dirks gives his impression that the Franeker varieties (especially pl.B, 15-27) were perfectly conserved, à fleur de coin, and of very pure silver.[25] The one exactly similar coin that has been analysed chemically (below) was found to be only 82 per cent fine, with 0.4 per cent tin. Another variety (below), which was not represented in the hoard but which is on a large flan and seems to be related to Dirks, pl.B, 15-19, is 90 per cent fine, without any tin. A later variety of B, 15-19 with unseriffed crosslets, is only 42 per cent fine, with over 3 per cent tin. There is a very similar find from Bidford-on-Avon, Warwicks, also of low weight.[26] There is no reason to think that these are English imitations: they are better interpreted as reflecting a severe decline at a later date than the t.p.q. of the Franeker hoard.

[25] Dirks, op.cit., pp.70f., note 4.
[26] 0.88g. Found in June 1987 by Mr. R. Laight and recorded by Mr. W. A. Seaby, Coin Register, 1987/56.

V

The porcupines in the portion of the Franeker hoard which passed originally to the Frisian Society comprise three distinct varieties, in unequal quantities, namely Metcalf Varieties B (21), E (60), and F (71).

FIG. Porcupine varieties of the Franeker phase. Variety B, modelled on the VICO variety. (After Dirks, pl.B, 23; pl.A, 11; pl.B, 14.)

Variety B, which is closely modelled on the early VICO variety, has three or occasionally four parallel lines under the curve of the porcupine, and a triangle below. On the reverse, the lop-sided square Ⅽ is replaced by an Ⅼ (Dirks, pl.B, 21, 23) or a long cross (pl.A, 11, 12 or, with lateral reversal, B, 13-14, 22). The outer border is distinctively ornamented with rows of pellets.

FIG. Porcupine varieties of the Franeker phase. Variety B, by another hand. (After Dirks, pl.A, 10 and B, 20.)

Dirks A, 10 and B, 20 (together, 3 specimens), while formally also of Variety B, have a different border, and the letter Ⅰ of VICO is in the early form of three joined pellets. On the obverse, B, 20 has a rectangle rather than a triangle. These specimens are no doubt the work of a different die-cutter.

FIG. Porcupine varieties of the Franeker phase. Variety E, modelled on Variety G. With 4 Is on the reverse (after Dirks, pl.B, 27), and with 2 Ls and 2 Is (Dirks, pl.B, 25).

Variety E copies the obverse detail of the earlier Variety G, with a rectangle beneath the curve. On some specimens it can be seen to contain an X (Dirks, pl.B, 24-7). The design in the reverse standard varies. Boldly engraved coins with four Is and two pellets (B, 26-7) are perhaps earlier than those with one or two Ls. The outer border is ornamented with a bold inverted letter T.

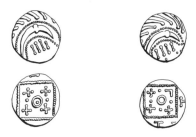

FIG. Porcupine varieties of the Franeker phase. Variety F. (After Dirks, pl.B, 16 and 18.)

Variety F has a fat, crescent-like curve outlined with fine pellets. The large pellet superimposed on the curve is sometimes more like a ring. The reverse has four crosslets, pommee, around the central annulet (Dirks, pl.B, 15-17, 62 specimens) or three crosslets and an L (B, 18-19, 9 specimens). The symbols are usually interspersed with either two or four pellets (pl.B, 15, no pellets, 9 specimens; 16, two pellets, 37 specimens; 17, four pellets, 16 specimens. B, 18 and 19, with an L, have four pellets.) A stylistic analysis, seeking to establish a correlation with the obverses, might be undertaken. The outer border of the reverse always has an inverted T.

FIG. Porcupine varieties of the Franeker phase. After Dirks A, 6 (hybrid?) and A, 4 and 8 (imitating Variety F).

Dirks A, 1 and 6 are hybrids, with the outlined spine and the reverse pattern of Variety F, but the pellet on the end of the spine, the triangle, and the reverse border ornament of Variety B. If they belong with either, it will be with B.

Dirks A, 4 and 8-9 imitate Variety F, not very robustly. They have widely-spaced quills, a different reverse design (TOT/– –), and simple lines in the border.

Dirks A, 2, 3, and 5 are possibly strays surviving from the Kloster Barthe phase.

What was the chronological pattern of Varieties B, E, and F? They may have been struck in that order or they may have been concurrent. The B/F hybrids point to an overlap at least in their circulation. Only Variety F, so far as is known, occurs in a debased alloy (c. 40 per cent, with unseriffed crosslets). There is another scarce variant, on which the central annulet is replaced by another crosslet, making five crosslets. There is at least one specimen of this variant, which was apparently not represented in Franeker, in the Koninklijk Penningkabinett. Its alloy and its status are otherwise unknown.

The Wijk-bij-Duurstede hoard was said to contain Varieties E and F, but was much too small (6 specimens) for the absence of B to be statistically significant.

The collections in the Middleburg Museum, with a presumed Domburg provenance, include the same range of Franeker varieties in roughly the same proportions as the hoard.

VI

The view of the later porcupines that has been sketched, tentatively, is of two phases. In the Kloster Barthe phase (c.710-15 to c.735 or later?) the typology of the coins is confused but their intrinsic value and reliability are by no means correspondingly unsatisfactory. The modal weight remains at the primary level, and thus higher than almost all other secondary sceattas. The alloy seems at first to have been maintained at around 90 per cent silver or better (on the evidence of the English single finds), but then to have fallen to *c.*80 per cent or even lower. The currency, which was prolific, may have included a proportion of copies, but they seem (from the metrology in conjunction with one's impression of style) not to have been numerous.

The Franeker phase (from *c.*735 or later, for a relatively short period?) begins with some sort of reform, by which porcupines on larger flans were struck, in a more orderly manner, as in the primary phase. There seems to have been a weight-reduction of around 5 per cent, but the evidence to define it precisely has not yet been published. There are, likewise, far too few chemical analyses to show in detail what happened with the alloy: it seems to have been maintained at around 80-90 per cent, except perhaps at the very end of the series, when there may have been a brief phase of severe debasement, shortly before the reforms of Pepin.

The porcupines remained an exceptionally strong currency almost to the end.

SERIES E, TYPE 53
(PORCUPINE / STEPPED CROSS)

A DERIVATIVE of the porcupine type, of which a miniature corpus of 8 specimens has been published by Blackburn and Bonser,[1] has an original cruciform reverse design, which is conventionally described as a stepped cross. The obverse is clearly inspired by Variety G. The acute angle which suggested the leg of an insect, the pellets superimposed on the spine, and the rectangular box-like arrangement beneath the porcupine are all echoed. The type is now known from nearly twenty specimens,

which are all or almost all from different dies. The weights of the heaviest reach 1.2-1.3g, but most specimens are distinctly lighter, at $c.$1.0-1.1g, – more in the range of G4. The alloy, nevertheless, is generally excellent (five analyses, 94, 94, 94, 90, and $c.$96 per cent,[2] two with a minute trace of tin).

Why was Type 53, which appears to march with the early porcupines, absent from Aston Rowant? The growing canon of specimens makes it seem increasingly unlikely that it was a small issue, which by chance was not represented in the hoard. Does it (just) post-date it? And is it continental, or is it an English version comparable with, say, Series T? (These are the constant questions 'when' and 'where', slightly elaborated). In an attempt to reach a judgement, we can set the type into

---

[1] M. A. S. Blackburn and M. J. Bonser, 'Single finds of Anglo-Saxon and Norman coins–2', *BNJ* 55 (1985), 55-78, at no.62, listing 8 known specimens. To these 8 can be added a specimen from the Stephanik collection, a BM coin ex Barnett, one specimen each in Paris and Brussels, and finds from Thetford, Watton, Caistor, Bradford Peverall, Hamwic and Saint-Bauzille. A specimen offered by Spinks in $c.$1984 may be one of the above.

[2] A fifth EPMA result of 76 per cent 'silver' with 1.7 per cent tin, has almost certainly been mixed up with that referring to another coin. The specimen allegedly 76 per cent fine is stylistically early. It was previously analysed by XRF (0.44), which showed a more believable 96 per cent 'silver'.

the same context of argument as has been worked out for the four early varieties of porcupines. The English single finds, which have a widespread distribution reminiscent of Varieties D and G, number at least eight. They come from Hamwic[3] and Bradford Peverell (near Dorchester, Dorset);[4] and from Witnesham, Suffolk, the Thetford district, Watton, Norfolk,[5] Caistor-by-Norwich, and Six Hills, on the line of the Fosse Way north of Leicester. *BMC* 199, with a pedigree through Dymock, is in all probability an English find and it has been suggested that it may be from Reculver or Thanet.[6] Continental finds are two from Domburg[7] and one from Maurik,[8] one in a hoard from the province of Friesland before 1904 (the Stephanik hoard),[9] one from the Kloster Barthe hoard,[10] one each in Paris and Brussels without provenance, but probably continental finds,[11] one from Cimiez[12] and another from the south of France, from Saint-Bauzille-de-Montmel (Hérault).[13]

The ratio of English to Domburg finds, at 8 to 2, is appreciably different from the combined totals of 73 to 63 for the four early varieties of porcupines. To match that ratio, one would be looking for about 7 finds of Type 53 at Domburg, not 2. Moreover the type is so readily identifiable and has until recently been so scarce that one may be confident that the reporting of it is virtually complete. On the statistics, it would be reasonable to hesitate over an English or continental attribution, and perhaps to defer judgement. The distribution-pattern in England, however, is too widespread for an English attribution to be plausible. The region of origin could only be in East Anglia, but if it were, one would not expect two finds from the Hampshire basin.

On balance, therefore, one should favour the simpler hypothesis, that Type 53 is continental. The unusual English/Domburg ratio might be, of course, because the type was produced somewhere other than at the mint-place of the four early varieties. It may, on the other hand, merely add to the enigma of distinctive variants of a basic design, minted

---

[3] A coin excavated since the publication of the Hamwic monograph. 1.01g.

[4] Found November 1989.

[5] Information by courtesy of Mr. Bonser.

[6] Blackburn and Bonser, loc.cit.

[7] W. Op den Velde, W. J. de Boone, and A. Pol, 'A survey of sceatta finds from the Low Countries', in *Sceattas in England and on the Continent*, pp.117-45, at p.141.

[8] W. Op den Velde, 'Sceattas gevonden bij Maurik en Rijswijk', *JMP* 69 (1982), 5-19, no.15, 0.77g.

[9] Op den Velde, de Boone, and Pol, loc.cit., at

p.143. The Stephanik specimen is now in the Ashmolean, ex Baldwin, and is catalogued below.

[10] Kloster Barthe (1838), 7503/7 II 7, 1.28g. Hill, ELM (=MLM) 694.

[11] The Brussels coin has a laterally reversed obverse.

[12] Le Gentilhomme 39. 1.20g.

[13] I am indebted to M.Jean-Claude Richard for photographs of this specimen, published in J. Lafaurie, 'Trésor de Nohanent et sceattas dé-couverts à Saint Bauzille de Montmel et à Sens', *Bull.de la Soc.Fr.de Num.* 1957, 99f.

concurrently in the Rhine mouths area. In default of a great deal more evidence from the Low Countries, there seems to be no way to pursue the problem.

The date of origin of Type 53 may be a few years later than the origin of the four substantive varieties – perhaps just before the date of concealment of Aston Rowant. Single specimens are reported in the slighly later hoards of Cimiez and Kloster Barthe, although their evidence for dating is ambiguous: these coins could have been old when hoarded.

We should be satisfied with a provisional verdict.

I

The style of the porcupine varies. The finest and most elaborate specimen includes two pelletted annulets in the obverse design. Others have only one, or an empty annulet, or even just a pellet. The reverse is often ornamented with pellets, in various combinations – one in each angle of the cross, or three, or four, or one in each angle and one in each arm of the cross. The better coins tend to be more elaborate, but there is as yet no clear correlation. One specimen has only a small x in one angle. Outside the dotted border there may be another circle of closely or widely spaced pellets, or a zig-zag outer border. Again, it is impossible to establish a correlation. One's instinct will be to arrange the coins into some sort of order in conformity with the general quality of their style, placing the specimens with pelletted annulets first.

TWO RARE PORCUPINE 'MULES'

Two RARE varieties listed by Hill as Type 4 var. (his pl.6, 27) and as a Type 12/5 'mule' (pl.6,13) both have a laterally reversed porcupine as one of their designs. One specimen of the former and two of the latter are known. Their attribution is inevitably uncertain. The 12/5 'mule' is known from a continental find and, not having turned up in England among the many finds of recent years, is probably continental. Type 4 var. may also be continental. One specimen of each is catalogued below, and they have been chemically analysed by EPMA.

I

Type 4 var. is perhaps copied from an early porcupine of Variety G. The other side of the coin has a four-letter inscription which has been read as

SEDE, but the D is very uncertain. In the margin there is a pseudo-legend. The coin is 91 per cent 'silver', with 0.25 per cent tin. One is at a loss to comment on it.

II

Dirks published a specimen of Type 12/5 as belonging to the Hallum hoard. Philip Hill suggests that it is an intruder in the hoard. If its obverse, reading ELVNDOИIΛ+, is copied from Series L (rather than *vice versa*) a Hallum provenance would impose either an unacceptably early date for Type 12, or an unacceptably late date for the hoard. The Ashmolean specimen is 25 per cent 'silver', with 5.6 per cent tin. It is from the same dies as the specimen in the Fries Museum.[1]

The suggestion, made by Philip Hill and followed by subsequent scholars, that the 12/5 'mule' is related to Series T, i.e. that it is from the same workshop, seems quite unwarranted.

[1] This can be seen from Dr. D. Hill's enlarged photograph, LFM 276.

BMC TYPE 10

NINE OR TEN genuine specimens are known of a hybrid type which 'mules' two obverses: a runic *æpa* or *apa*, probably copied from Series D, Type 2c rather than directly from Type C2, and a porcupine-related obverse imitated from Series E, Variety G3 or G4, with the mature legend TILV or something similar. A corpus has been published by Op den Velde.[1]

One or possibly two specimens are reported from Domburg, but there were none in the Aston Rowant and Remmerden hoards. Doubt has been cast on the authenticity of the only (alleged) stray find of recent years from England.[2] The Escharen hoard of 1980, in which there were four specimens, together with five of Type 2c which made up the rest of the hoard, is thus the first substantial source of information about the type.

It would come as no great surprise if one were to discover a die-link between Type 10 and Type 2c, but one would be rash, in that case, to jump to the conclusion that Type 10 was from the same mint as 2c. A more prudent hypothesis would be that the mint of Type 10 was eclectic, and that the specimen apparently of Type 2c was imitative. We may assume, in view of the Escharen hoard, that Type 10 belongs to the Low Countries, and to a small mint where the influence of both Series D and E was recognized. Tiel has been suggested, but Op den Velde comments that there is no justification.

Two pairs of coins linked by their obverse dies, in each case with different reverses, confirm that the bust with runic *æpa* was indeed on the lower die and – more interestingly – suggest that the normal practice was to use more than one reverse with an obverse die. Statistical estimation will suffer from very wide margins of imprecision, and it will be no more than a rough guess to think of 20 obverses and 30-50 reverses.

The extreme scarcity of the type, particularly in England, may be

[1] W. Op den Velde, 'Escharen 1980', *JMP* 72 (1985), 5-12.

[2] The writer accepted it when he saw it in 1982 but had no reason to be suspicious: D. M. Metcalf, 'A Frisian sceat of eclectic design from Long Wittenham, Oxon., possibly minted at Tiel', in *Sceattas in England and on the Continent*, pp.194f., with line-drawing. The weight is acceptable.

merely a measure of the overwhelming quantities in which Series D and E were produced; but it is possible that the TILV coins tended to have a rather more localized circulation than those of the major mints.

The heaviest specimens weigh *c*.1.25-1.30g, which suggests a relatively early date of origin. Die-duplicates can vary, however: Escharen 7 and 8 weigh 1.245 and 1.11g.

Escharen 6 may well stand near the head of the series. Its obverse is

particularly neat, and the reverse has not yet fully assumed the characteristic 'man in the moon' facial appearance. Nor has the legend settled down into the normal TILV.

The quills are tightly packed and neat, with inconspicuous pellets, on

the heavier coins. Escharen 7 has larger pellets, and an annulet added to the design.

Op den Velde b and a seem to be the latest members in the stylistic sequence. The radiate crown of the prototype is reduced to a steeply-angled or curved[3] diadem. The weights are 1.20 and 1.04g respectively, and the curve of the porcupine is modelled to represent the cheek or jaw. The Long Wittenham find (1.13g), if it is genuine, belongs closely with Op den Velde b.

The sequence thus appears to divide roughly into two, with a linear curve, copied from the porcupine, giving way to a modelled face – a stylistic transition eagerly sought by earlier scholars, but here in the reverse order from the one they tended to assume. There is probably a downward drift in weight, but there is no sign of the dual weight-standard of Type 2c. No chemical analyses have been undertaken. A suggested order is Escharen 6, Escharen 9(h) = d/e (probably one coin), Escharen 7 = 8, i, c, b, a.

---

[3] Lindsay's line-drawing, reproduced by Op den Velde, is not as accurate as it might be, and the reader should use the illustration in *BMC*, pl.2, 13.

I

Specimen g in Op den Velde's corpus weighs 1.60g. It is evidently a (modern) cast forgery. Suspicion also falls on f (the Grantley coin), of which the weight is again excessive, at 1.52g.[4]

[4] Spink Auction 20, 31 March 1982, lot 45 (23.5 grains).

'MADELINUS' DENARII (SERIES Ma)

THE COPIOUS series of tremisses of the moneyer Madelinus, naming Dorestad as their mint, have been classified by Mrs. Zadoks-Josephus Jitta, who suggested that the type was eventually copied or continued elsewhere than Dorestad, presumably somewhere further to the north-east, in Frisia.[1] The series as a whole has been mapped by Op den Velde, de Boone, and Pol, who demonstrate a heavy concentration of the gold in Friesland, but with finds also in the Rhine valley, and in Belgium.[2]

FIG. 'Madelinus' tremissis. Caistor-by-Norwich find.

Interpreting the map presents analogous problems to interpreting, for example, the map of porcupine finds: the landscape of Friesland is such that it seems unlikely to have been the location of a major mint.

The series terminates with very scarce coins which are of the same design but in silver, and sometimes debased silver. The 'Madelinus' type thus apparently spans the transition from gold to silver, without alteration of type, in much the same way as the coinages of Pada and Vanimundus (and, apparently, Series F and even A). They may neatly be given the label Ma, to match Pa and Va. Grierson and Blackburn treat them as sceattas, in spite of their generally Merovingian appearance.[3] As regards the gold tremisses of Madelinus, they query the argument from style,[4] pointing out that Zadoks-Josephus Jitta's copies may be merely the work of an inferior die-cutter at the same mint; and the same comment would carry over to the denarii too.

So far, so good; but when we try to set the 'Madelinus' denarii into a wider context, new problems emerge. Why are they so scarce in

[1] A. N. Zadoks-Josephus Jitta, 'De eerste munt-slag te Duurstede', *JMP* 48 (1961), 1-14.

[2] W. Op den Velde, W. J. de Boone, and A. Pol, 'A survey of sceatta finds from the Low Countries', in *Sceattas in England and on the Continent*', pp.117-45, Map 3 (at p.123), and p.122.

[3] *MEC*, p.151.

[4] ibid., p.137.

comparison with the tremisses, and why are they so scarce in comparison with the primary porcupines? Why are they unrepresented in the early hoards? Did their issue quickly cease? Could they have been superseded at Dorestad by the first porcupines? – That is problematic, both because Series Ma shows debasement, and because even specimens of good silver are not of consistently high weight.

I

Apart from the negative evidence of their absence from the hoards and their scarcity generally among finds from the Netherlands, there are two important sources of information which contribute to our understanding of when and where the 'Madelinus' denarii were minted. A hoard from near Wittnau, from the mountain fortress of the Wittnauer Horn, among the alpine passes of Switzerland, comprised four specimens together with

three of the 'interlace' type and one Merovingian coin from the region of Tours.[5] It is manifestly a traveller's hoard, which creates a presumption that the 'Madelinus' and 'interlace' coins had been carried south together, from a region where both were available. That certainly suggests the Meuse valley: the fact that 'Madelinus' coins (in gold) are commonly found in Frisia is no more (or less) a reason for thinking that they were minted there, than it is in the case of the 'interlace' or 'star of David' denarii.[6]

The four 'Madelinus' coins were analysed by Voûte in the laboratory of the Schweizerisches Landesmuseum, Zurich. They were found to contain 94, 92, 77, and 46 per cent silver respectively. The method of analysis is not recorded, but was presumably XRF or SEM. The style of the fourth coin led Geiger to suggest that it might be a contemporary counterfeit. We cannot rule out that possibility, and the only firm evidence of debasement in the official series, therefore, comes from the coin with 77 per cent silver. It is slender evidence from which to query an early date for the type. Yet, unless it is very early, it can hardly be from

[5] H.-U. Geiger, 'Ein kleiner frühmittelalterlicher Münzschatz vom Wittnauer Horn', *Archäologie der Schweiz* 3 (1980), 56-8.

[6] See the discussion of those types, below.

Dorestad. If it were from a mint in the Meuse valley, irregularity of weight and alloy at an early date might be more credible.

The 'interlace' coins in the hoard have been taken as evidence of a later date of concealment. Their silver contents are 79, 70, and 46 per cent. That has led to the suggestion, in *MEC*, that they were added to an earlier accumulation of coins.[7] With what seems so clearly to be a traveller's hoard, that surely is special pleading.

The 'interlace' type is present already in Hallum, and Wittnau could be from about the same time. Debasement in the English sceattas offers no certain guidance as to date, (witness the discussion of Series K and L) and we should hesitate to assume that it does so on the Continent.

II

Two die-duplicate 'Madelinus' denarii were excavated at Dankirke, in Jutland.[8] The site also yielded a pale gold tremissis of the same type. The chronological range of coin-finds from Dankirke begins earlier than at

nearby Ribe. There is some encouragement, therefore, to think that the 'Madelinus' coins could be early. But the site has also yielded later sceattas. Its evidence cannot, therefore, exclude a later date.

The presence of two coins of Series D and the absence of any early porcupines at Dankirke, in a rather small sample, points towards a mint-place other than Dorestad for the 'Madelinus' denarii, but it is no more than a straw in the wind.

Geiger notes the absence of pellets to left and right of the cross, on the coin with only 46 per cent silver, which he is inclined to see as imitative; but the Dankirke finds lack the pellets too.

III

The available answers to the questions 'when' and 'where' are inadequate. In these circumstances, one may emphasize the absence of

[7] *MEC*, p.151.

[8] M. Bencard (editor), *Ribe Excavations, 1970-76*, vol.1, 'Sceattas and other coin finds', by K. Ben-dixen, at pp.99-101. The weights are 0.88 and 0.76g (broken).

'Madelinus' denarii at Domburg, and also in England.

The scale of their issue is unclear: the die-duplicates at Dankirke may well have arrived there together, having stayed together since minting. If the type were from the Meuse valley, for example, it might be under-represented at Domburg. A Frisian origin in the Utrecht region might also deserve consideration.

WHERE WERE THE SO-CALLED 'HERSTAL' AND 'MAASTRICHT' TYPES MINTED?

Two marginal sceatta types occur in some quantities in the Hallum and Franeker hoards, and also (in quite different relative proportions) among the Domburg and Dorestad site-finds. Singletons are on record from half a dozen other sites, and the 'Herstal' type is said to have been found frequently along the Meuse valley.[1] Both types evidently belong to the Low Countries or to Frisia, but it is difficult, from the available evidence, to locate either of them more precisely. Neither of the traditional attributions, to Herstal (near Liège) and Maastricht respectively, commands support at the present day.[2] The list of continental finds[3] is as follows:

	'Herstal'	'Maastricht'
Hallum hoard	24 (10%)	2 (<1%)
Franeker hoard	36 (8%)	1 (<1%)
Föhr hoard	1	1 (2?)
Domburg	23 (2%)	19 (2%)
Dorestad	8 (14%)	6 (10%)
Dorestad hoard, 1846	0	2 (25%)
Rijswijk	1	1
Wageningen	-	1
Friesland	1	-
Namur	1	-
Tournai	-	1

[1] L. de Coster, 'Considérations à propos de quelques deniers inédits de Pépin le bref et de Charlemagne', *Revue de Numismatique Belge*, 3rd. Series, 3 (1859), 210-38, at pp.213-15 and pl.7, 1-2.

[2] *MEC* pp.149-54.

[3] The list is drawn from W. Op den Velde, W. J. de Boone, and A. Pol, 'A survey of sceatta finds from the Low Countries', in *Sceattas in England and on the Continent*, edited by D. Hill and D. M. Metcalf, Oxford, 1984, pp.117-45; H. Frère, 'Les monnaies mérovingiennes du pays mosan', in *La Civilisation mérovingienne dans le bassin mosan*, edited by M. Otte and J. Willems, Liège, 1986, at pp.269-79 (a recent find excavated in the place Saint-Lambert, Liège); V. Zedelius, 'Neue Sceattas aus dem Rheinland – Bonn und Xanten –', *Zeitschrift für Archäologie des Mittelalters* 8 (1980), 139-52.

Meuse valley	x	-
Liège (Saint-Lambert)	-	1
Xanten	-	1
Krefeld-Gellep	-	1
Wittnauer Horn hoard	-	3

There is an anomaly in the above statistics, in that the 'Herstal' type far outweighs the 'Maastricht' type in the Frisian hoards, whereas the two types are found in very comparable quantities at both Domburg and Dorestad. Also, both are relatively far more common at Dorestad than at Domburg. The practical starting-point is to devise an explanation for those contrasts. It might be along the lines that the 'Herstal' type is from a mint-place much closer to Frisia, or even in Frisia; or there might be a partly chronological explanation; or the alloy of the coins might make one more suitable for hoarding than the other. As both types are already present in the Hallum hoard, their issue must have begun by c.720.

I

The designs of the 'Herstal' type are among the simplest and least accomplished: a six-pointed star composed of two overlapping triangles (and often described as a 'seal of Solomon' or a 'star of David'[4]) with a cross in the centre, and pellets in some but not all of the angles. The reverse has a particularly untidy and lop-sided design, with radiating

FIG. Star ('Herstal') type.

strokes around a central cross, an initial cross, and pellets between some of the strokes, at random but often in three or four consecutive spaces.

[4] *MEC*, p.152; H. H. Völckers, *Karolingische Münzfunde der Frühzeit (751-800)*, Göttingen, 1965, p.62.

[5] This can be seen from Dr. Hill's photos.

The collection in the Fries Museum, of specimens from Hallum and Franeker, contains few instances of die-duplication.[5] The issue was clearly a large one.

Two specimens in the Grierson collection were analysed by XRF and found to contain 81 and 82 per cent 'silver' respectively, with 2.0 and 2.4 per cent tin.[6]

De Coster, as long ago as 1859, saw in these and similar denarii with A as one of their types a punning reference, in the star, to the palace of Aristalium (Herstal),[7] – a locality now submerged in the outskirts of Liège. Pepin II, who was mayor of the Austrasian palace from 679 and controlled Neustria from 687, is known to historians as 'Pepin of Herstal', but that seems to be essentially anachronistic and mistaken. Herstal was one of a number of palaces used by the Carolingians in the ninth century. At the probable date of issue of the 'star' type, the power-base of the rulers of Austrasia lay further south.

The distribution of finds suggests a place of origin more accessible to Dorestad than to Domburg. The Frisian hoards should probably be disregarded as *Auslandsfunde*, and more weight given to the stray finds from Namur and (reportedly) the Meuse valley generally, on the grounds that the 'star' type makes up a higher proportion of the finds from that district than it does, for example, in Frisia. Völckers sees the linear or geometric style as reason for proposing a Flemish origin,[8] but the only single-find which could be held to support his suggestion is the one from Tournai. The type is absent along the Belgian coast.

It is puzzling that there is so little difference in style between the Hallum and Franeker specimens, given the difference in date of deposit of the two hoards.[9] A classification of the 'star' type, taking account of weight and alloy, may eventually make the sequence of dies clear.

It may help to make clear, also, whether a somewhat similar type with linear designs, present in both hoards, (Hallum, Dirks, pl. D, 24, and

FIG. Star ('Herstal') related type: Hallum, Dirks pl. D 24 and Franeker, Dirks pl.C, 34.

[6] *MEC*, 636-7; D. M. Metcalf, 'Interpreting the alloy of the Merovingian silver coinage', in *Studies in Numismatic Method*, edited by C. N. L. Brooke et al., Cambridge, 1983, pp.113-26, nos.42-3.

[7] De Coster, loc.cit. (note 1 above).

[8] Völckers, op.cit (note 4 above).

[9] The history of the Hallum hoard (1866) and the Franeker hoard (1868) is rehearsed in J. Dirks, *Les*

Franeker, pl.C, 34) is related. Lafaurie has suggested that another type, in similar style, is the forerunner of the 'star' type.[10]

II

The 'interlace' type, composed as a quatrefoil knot, similar to the triquetra, was formerly attributed to Maastricht because of its affiliation to a similar early Carolingian type. That the Merovingian and early Carolingian 'interlace' coins are from the same mint, we need not doubt. It does not help us much, however, because the attribution of the Carolingian coins is, if anything, more uncertain than that of the preceding sceattas. The RF on the obverse of the deniers with 'interlace' reverse is distorted and reversed. With imagination, it can be made to read (after a fashion) TR, and this has been construed as *Triectum* or *Traiectum ad Moesum*, for Maastricht (rather than *Traiectum*, for Utrecht). There is another series of early Carolingian coins, with a clear letter T added between the letters RP, and with the Frisian *strijdbijl* or axe, for which a Utrecht origin has been canvassed.[11] The political status of Utrecht at the likely date of issue of the 'interlace' sceattas needs to be taken into account.

The type has been found in association with the 'star' sceattas in the Hallum and Franeker hoards, and at Domburg and Dorestad. It is, again, relatively far more plentiful at Dorestad than Domburg, and is represented in the hoards only by one or two specimens. Stray finds from Tournai, Liège, Xanten, and Krefeld-Gellep suggest an origin away from the North Sea coasts, perhaps in the lower Meuse valley.

The issue has been very thoroughly studied by Zedelius.[12] He distinguished coins in coarse style (his illustration A), and an *Ausführung* (his B), mostly on thinner flans and in lower relief. There are other variants: the specimen in the (late) Föhr hoard has a right-facing head, and a second hybrid *dans le commerce* is probably also from Föhr.[13] Op den Velde and De Boone have studied the iconography of the ring-

---

Anglo-Saxons et leurs petits deniers dits sceattas, Brussels, 1870, at pp.56, note 2 and 58, note 3. In view of the short time between the discovery of the two hoards, not far apart, it must cross one's mind to wonder whether false information was given about the second lot of 'star' deniers. Future study of the coins in the Leeuwarden Museum may help to clarify the facts.

[10] *MEC* 638, with silver contents of 92 per cent.

There is a specimen in Brussels, *RBN* 128 (1982), pl.11, 123.

[11] D. M. Metcalf, 'Artistic borrowing, imitation, and forgery in the eighth century', *Hamburger Beiträge zur Numismatik* 20 (1966), 379-92.

[12] Zedelius, loc.cit (note 3 above), with enlarged illustrations of five specimens.

[13] ibid., p.150, n.60.

FIG. Interlace ('Maastricht') coins: Zedelius Types A and B.

ornament or interlace, and have proposed a similar classification into Type I, IIA, and IIB.[14] Type I (the smallest group) has a naturalistic head, facing either left or right. It is reminiscent of Series G. Type II is grossly schematized. The head is always left-facing, and is divided by Op den Velde and De Boone into IIA in bold relief with thick lines, (i.e. Zedelius variety A), and IIB in more delicate style and with less pronounced relief (Zedelius, B). The Hallum[15] and Franeker[16] specimens are of Types IIB and IIA respectively, and the Xanten and Krefeld-

FIG. Interlace ('Maastricht') coins: the Hallum hoard specimens, Dirks pl.D, 16 and Hill photo 271.

FIG. Interlace ('Maastricht') type: the Franeker hoard, Dirks, pl.C, 37.

Gellep finds are also of Type IIA. There seems not to be any sharp division in terms of style between B and A, which were perhaps struck in that order.

The Wittnauer Horn hoard contained three specimens, which again tend to blur the division between B and A. Two of them have a cluster of 5 pellets behind the head; these obverse dies are associated with rather blunt and clumsy interlace patterns.

[14] W. Op den Velde and W. J. de Boone, 'Het raadsel van het ringenornament', *Westerheem* 32 (1983), 355-64.

[15] Dirks lists two specimens (p.57) and illustrates one (pl.D, 16). The Fries Museum specimen, Inventory no.FM 271 (Hill photos, 271) appears to be the other, unless Dirks's line-drawing is rather

inaccurate. Hill 271 is the basis of the line-drawing published by Op den Velde and de Boone to exemplify Type IIB.

[16] Dirks, pl.C, 37, Inv.FM 318 (Zedelius, p.150) = Hill photo 319, certainly the coin illustrated by Dirks. It is of Type IIA.

259

FIG. Interlace ('Maastricht') type: the Wittnauer Horn hoard.

There is a cluster of problems arising from the suggested scheme of classification. The Hallum coins, which are from the earlier hoard, are of Type IIB, which stands at the end of the proposed sequence. That would imply that the issue was largely complete by *c.*720. Secondly, it is difficult to assign all known specimens to one or other of the three types or sub-types. Zedelius, in a more recent article, has gone so far as to hint at a division between Merovingian prototype and Frisian copies.[17] (The find from the Tournai region is in devolved but regular style. It weighs 1.15g and is described as being of copper alloy.)

If there was any copying, however, it may have been in the other direction. The coin with a helmeted bust in the Hallum hoard, Dirks pl.D, 17, which might be considered as a specimen of Type I, could equally well be derivative from the substantive issue, Type II.

FIG. Interlace ('Maastricht') copy: Dirks, pl.D, 17.

Information about the alloy offers the best prospect of resolving the ambiguities. The two specimens in *MEC* have been analysed by XRF. The first, which is of Type IIA, and very similar to the Franeker specimen, is 88 per cent 'silver' with 1.5 per cent tin.[18] The reverse die, in particular, of Wittnauer Horn no.4 is again similar: it is the best of the

[17] V. Zedelius, 'Eighth-century archaeology in the Meuse and Rhine valleys: a context for the sceatta finds', in *Coinage in Ninth-Century Northumbria*, edited by D. M. Metcalf, Oxford, 1987, pp.403-13. (This paper was read at the Seventh Oxford Symposium, and should have been published in 1984, but through an editorial fault was not.)

Zedelius advances the hypothesis that the coins in the Franeker hoard, in fresh condition, had been carefully chosen, and he goes on to remark that the 'Maastricht' specimen seems to be an early rather than a late variety. He notes the wide range of silver contents of the type.

[18] *MEC* 634; Metcalf (note 6 above) 34.

three specimens in the hoard, with 79 per cent silver. The other two have 70 and 46 per cent silver. The second coin in *MEC*, which is stylistically more devolved, the neck being reduced more or less to a vertical line, is 43 per cent 'silver' with 5.6 per cent tin.[19] Two more specimens have been analysed by EPMA. One, which is an English find from near Oxford, may well be imitative: it is 74 per cent 'silver', with 2.8 per cent tin.[20] The other is clearly of Type IIA, and contains roughly 45 per cent 'silver' (or less?) with 1.1 per cent tin – thus matching *MEC* 635.[21] If one may venture to generalize from such limited information as these four analyses provide, it seems that there was wide variation in the silver contents even within Type IIA.

The Dutch royal collection contains at least 8 identifiable specimens, of

FIG. Interlace ('Maastricht') type: HPK 497, 498, 492, and 287.

which two are of Type IIB (one being very similar to the Hallum coin),[22] and 6 are of Type IIA.[23] There are four specimens in Brussels, of Types IIA (3) and (apparently) IIB.[24]

III

The 'star' and 'interlace' types hardly qualify as sceattas. They have in the past been accepted as such, partly because their occurrence in the Hallum and Franeker hoards made a Frisian attribution seem plausible. The region where they are relatively most plentiful, however, seems to be the lower Meuse valley, and that is the best guess that we can make at their place of origin.

[19] *MEC* 635; Metcalf 35.

[20] Catalogued below.

[21] Previously analysed by XRF as O.126 (*JMP* 55, 1968, 41). The EPMA silver measurement was qualified as having been affected by corrosion.

[22] HPK 497 (cf. Hallum 271) and 498.

[23] HPK 492, 494, 17283, 17287, and (cruder) 495 and 17248.

[24] H. Vanhoudt, 'De merovingische munten in het Penningkabinet van de Koninklijke Bibliotheek te Brussel', *RBN* 128 (1982), 95-194, nos.258-61.

The find evidence, therefore, certainly does not rule out the traditional attributions to Herstal and Maastricht, even if it cannot, in principle, be expected to support them other than generally. The political circumstances of the two places in the 720s affect the plausibility of the attributions. Utrecht, where St. Willibrord went to meet King Redbad in 716, was evidently of sufficient importance to be a mint-place. Herstal is less obvious. The royal palace played a modest part in the task of minting in the second half of the ninth century, signing **PALATINA MONE**; and in the Merovingian period there are mints at places where there were palaces (which is not quite the same as demonstrably palatine mints). Whether Herstal was a place of much importance in the 710s and 720s is questionable. The attribution of a large-scale coinage to Herstal would be, if not contrary to expectation, at least unsupported by it. We should hesitate to go beyond the archaeological evidence.

THE WESTERN LIMITS OF THE SPREAD OF SCEATTAS IN NORMANDY

ROUEN was among the more prolific mints striking silver deniers in Merovingian style. Many of them have a distinctive facing head with pointed chin on the obverse, and a flower of six petals on the reverse. There was thus a recognizable currency associated with the town at the end of the seventh century and in the first quarter of the eighth: there was no monetary vacuum to be filled by sceattas. There is no occasion to imagine that any sceattas were minted in Rouen. Whether any circulated there is something that we can only know from the evidence of an assemblage of local finds.

It may appear to be an ambiguity in the evidence, that Rouen should lie beyond the zone where sceattas were the dominant currency, and yet that there should be a certain proportion of sceattas in hoards from beyond Rouen – at Bais, in Brittanny; south of the Loire at Saint-Pierre-les-Etieux; and even on the Gironde estuary at Plassac. Those hoards testify to the rapid diffusion of the deniers from many Merovingian mints, into western and south-western Gaul. Sceattas may have been carried past Rouen by merchants engaged in long-distance trade, who navigated the great highway of the River Seine – travelling, for example, as far as the fair at Saint-Denis. Any sceattas which were thus put into circulation in the Ile-de-France will have mingled with the local deniers in Merovingian style, and will have been accepted for their intrinsic value. They would seem to have made up no more than 5 per cent of the currency.

Not many deniers or sceattas are recorded as finds from Rouen and its region. Lafaurie in 1980 drew up, with the assistance of the departmental museum of antiquities, an inventory of all known finds from the fifth to the eighth centuries from Seine-Maritime.[1] The most plentiful category

[1] J. Lafaurie, 'Trouvailles de monnaies franques et mérovingiennes en Seine-Maritime (V^e-VIIe s.)', in *Histoire et numismatique en Haute-Normandie* (=Cahier des Annales de Normandie, 12A), edited by N. Gautier, Caen, 1980, pp.93-107.

are the scarce and interesting issues of the monastery of Saint-Ouen de Rouen. Almost all the known specimens are plated. They seem to be of relatively late date, leading directly into a coinage in early Carolingian style. Lafaurie suggests that they are from c.740-50, and that their production may have celebrated the re-naming of the abbey of Saint-Pierre, where the remains of St. Audoenus came to rest.[2] The obverse type bears a resemblance to Series G (for which an attribution to Quentovic is arguable). The reverse is a distinctive two-line inscription. Specimens have been found in Rouen, rue des Murs-Saint-Ouen, in 1860; rue des Basnages, in 1864; in the Seine near Rouen, betwen Bouille and Duclair; at Fécamp in excavations of the old castle;[3] at Laon; and at Domburg.

From the much longer period from c.680 to c.740 there is little to report. Again from Rouen itself, there is a porcupine sceat, found at the corner of rue de l'Hôtel-de-Ville and rue de l'Ecole, in 1864.[4] It is of a

FIG. Porcupine sceat: the Rouen find of 1864.

secondary variety, and is so eccentric in style that the question will arise whether it could be a copy made elsewhere than in the Rhine mouths area. No close comparanda have been found. The date is difficult to assess: perhaps the 720s or 730s.

A coin of Series H, Type 49, is recorded to have been found in the ruins of the abbey of Saint-Wandrille, close to the Seine some way downstream from Rouen.[5] It will no doubt have been carried across the Channel directly from Hamwic, on the facing coast. It is of Metcalf Variety 3. Its date of minting is again difficult to determine, but is

[2] id., 'Deniers du VIIIe siècle de Saint-Ouen de Rouen', *Bulletin de la Soc.fr.de num.*, Year 33 (1978), 368-72, for a full discussion of the type. The same text and illustrations are printed in the volume cited in note 1.

[3] id., Nouvelles découvertes de deniers mérovingiens à Fécamp (Seine-Maritime), ibid., Year 37

(1982), 134-7.

[4] *Monnaies, médailles, et jetons* (exhibition catalogue), Musée départemental des antiquitiés, Rouen, 1978, p.15, no.16 (plate 2).

[5] *SCBI Mack* 357 = Metcalf 73.3 in P. Andrews, editor, *The Coins and Pottery from Hamwic*.

unlikely to have been earlier than c.725.

Excavations since 1985, close to the cathedral, have yielded two interesting imitative coins.[6] The first is a copy of Series G, reproducing the standard reverse with its fours Xs in an accomplished and forceful style. One can see from the Xs that the coin is imitative: instead of being pommee they have elegantly flared limbs, truncated squarely. The obverse bust is reminiscent of Series G, but has a legend added. It reads ΔOITIᴧNA+ – an echo, possibly, of LVNDONIA+ in its lay-out, although it may have had some local meaning.

FIG. Excavation coins from Rouen, 1985.

The other find copies the normal obverse of Series G, 'muling' it with the interlace reverse of the so-called Maastricht type.

That appears to be the complete tally of finds.[7] One cannot help reflecting that if Seine-Maritime were part of the United Kingdom the record might be fuller. For the period c.680-c.620 we have a virtual absence of find-evidence, even though a considerable range of deniers was minted in Rouen, and can be dated to the two or three decades around 700 by the hoards in which they occur.

We should, perhaps, resist the obvious conclusion, and return an open verdict on the composition of the currrency of the lower Seine region in those years, until at least a few finds turn up. It should then become apparent which series of sceattas, if any, were regularly carried as far west as the mouth of the Seine.

[6] J. Pilet-Lemière and J. le Maho, 'Deux deniers du VIIIe s. dits "sceattas" découverts à Rouen', BSFN Year 45 (1990), 737-9.

[7] J. Delaporte and J. Lafaurie, 'Catalogue des monnaies', in La Neustrie, Les pays au nord de la Loire, de Dagobert à Charles le Chauve (VIIe-IXe siècle), edited by P. Périn and L.-C. Feffer, (Rouen), 1985, at pp.322-5.

SERIES G

THE MAIN PART of Series G consists of a single type (*BMC* Type 3a) with little formal variation. A date of origin not later than *c.*720 is proved by the Garton-on-the-Wolds grave-find and the Hallum and Cimiez hoards. A subsidiary part of the series comprises copies in crude style, the 3a obverse sometimes being muled with reverse types imitating Series J. There is, further, a fringe of copies of uncertain, perhaps continental, origin. Specimens of the main series are generally of very pure silver, while the alloy of the subsidiary and imitative coins varies from 50 down to 20 per cent silver or even less. The weights of the best coins are variable, but appear to be significantly less, at *c.*1.0–1.2g, than those of most English primary sceattas. The absence of Series G from the Aston Rowant and Bais hoards suggests, although it cannot completely prove, that the beginning of the issue was not earlier than *c.*710.

Series G was mistakenly interpreted in 1972[1] as belonging to west Sussex, on the basis of the unusually high proportion that it made up among the (rather few) finds from there. In the intervening years the list of English provenances has grown considerably. The type accounted for nearly 2 per cent of the single finds of the 1980s. While it remains true that G is over-represented in west Sussex (3 out of a dozen finds[2]), one can now see that the series has a very widespread distribution throughout eastern and midland England, with an emphasis on the north midlands and on Lincolnshire and Yorkshire, which puts an attribution to the little-monetized kingdom of the South Saxons quite out of the question.

A better hypothesis, offered in 1986,[3] is that Series G is continental. Sussex having been ruled out, there is no region of England to which, on the basis of a concentration of single finds, it could be convincingly assigned as a coinage minted in the decade 710-20. We are compelled, therefore, to look further afield. Series G cannot be from any mint-place

---

[1] D. M. Metcalf, 'The "bird and branch" sceattas in the light of a find from Abingdon', *Oxoniensia* 37 (1972), 51-65, at p.65.

[2] Pyecombe, Selsey, and Arundel.

[3] M. Biddle and others, 'Coins of the Anglo-Saxon period from Repton, Derbyshire, II', *BNJ* 56 (1986), 16-34.

MAP. Single finds of Series G. Round symbols: specimens which are certainly or probably in appropriate style. Triangles: various copies and imitations. The Garton-on-the-Wolds grave find is included. (24 specimens).

267

in the area of the Rhine mouths, for it makes up only 0.7 per cent of the Domburg finds – that is, much less than its representation in England. Apart from the Hallum hoard (which has an English element) it is virtually unknown among Low Countries provenances except for a single coin recovered as a grave-find at Wageningen. But there is a marked concentration of finds in the coastlands of northern France, from where there are in general very few sceattas on record; and the distinctive design is echoed in imitative pieces from Normandy.[4] Specimens of Series G have been found in excavations at the abbey of Corbie in Picardy (a crude imitation with only *c*.30 per cent silver),[5] at Térouanne, and at Étaples (a G/E imitation).[6] The special coinage of Saint-Ouen de Rouen has an obverse design not dissimilar to Series G.[7]   If Rouen itself can be excluded (as has been argued in the preceding section) the obvious candidate as a northern French mint-place for a substantial series of sceattas is Quentovic. It was a mint both for Merovingian gold (signed VVICCO, or VVIC IN PONTIO, and including issues by a moneyer Anglus) and for early Carolingian silver, but lacks any substantial coinage of Merovingian deniers. The wic was one of the main gateways through which English cross-Channel travellers entered and returned from Gaul. The *Vita Wilfridi* describes Quentovic in 678 as the 'via rectissima' from England to Rome. Customs dues were collected there, for which the abbot of Saint-Wandrille was at one stage the administrator; but its importance as a trading emporium was probably small in comparison with Dorestad.

There is an intriguing irregularity in the English find-evidence for Series G, where in view of the number of sites yielding G among a total of only three or four sceattas, the type seems to be under-represented at the major trading wics and other major productive sites. It is absent or virtually absent at Reculver, Tilbury, London, Barham, and Royston, and curiously scarce at Hamwic. That perhaps suggests that its mint-place was not a great trading centre (although once its coins had become mingled in general circulation in England, they would of course have been accepted on the basis of their intrinsic value and their reputation, and used for whatever purposes were required of coinage). Equally curious is the dual concentration of finds in west Sussex and northern

[4] See the preceding section.

[5] Excavated in 1982 by the Association des Amis du Vieux Corbie. I am indebted to Dr. E. A. Feest of AERE Harwell, who analysed the coin by XRF and found 30 per cent silver, 9 per cent tin, and 4.6 per cent lead. The coin was found in the foundations of the cloister, which had been disturbed in the building of a cellar in the nineteenth century.

[6] These are discussed and illustrated in D. M. Metcalf 'La traversée de la Manche (VIIIe–IXe siècles)', *BSFN* 1979, 511-15.

[7] See the preceding section.

France, and in Lincolnshire and Yorkshire. The northerly finds could in principal have arrived either by sea or overland through the midlands – or, of course, some by one route and some the other. There is a distinct absence of finds from East Anglia. That suggests that any maritime link was by way of the east-coast Frisian trade with York. Finds such as those from Six Hills, on the line of the Fosse Way, and from nearby Wymeswold, point to the use of overland routes.

The pattern of the English finds, in its positive and negative aspects, is closest to that for Series J, at much the same date. The distribution of Series G may be seen tentatively as a reflection of Quentovic's importance for England predominantly as a Channel port used in long-distance, non-commercial movements, e.g. pilgrimages, and journeys to Rome. What we see in the pattern of finds tends, as usual, to reveal the dominant factor in the spread of Series G: one should not suppose from the find-evidence that that was the only use of the type.

The hypothesis of Quentovic as the mint-place of Series G rests, then, on north French finds which, although few in total, make up a significant fraction of the regional assemblage; on a similar pattern in west Sussex, implying direct cross-Channel contacts; on an unusually scattered distribution of finds reaching northwards through the midlands and in the eastern coastlands (but not in East Anglia); and on good negative evidence from Rouen and from Domburg and the Low Countries generally.

Quentovic itself still keeps its secrets. The exact site of the wic had long been sought in the general vicinity of Étaples, before the recent and very promising excavations at Visemaretz began to reveal an archaeological site reminiscent, in its numerous rubbish pits, etc., of Hamwic. If the context of Series G was similar to that of Series H, major excavations at its mint-place might transform our data-base. We have large numbers of specimens of Series H, Types 39 and 49, nearly all of which come from the soil of Hamwic: without them, how sketchy our knowledge of those types would be! While Quentovic remained undiscovered, it may be that something comparable has been true of Series G. By a happy chance, the first sceat to be recovered in the excavations at Visemaretz, in 1987, was of Series G.[8] Further archaeological work there will no doubt eventually establish whether the site really is that of Quentovic – and whether Series G was conspicuous in the currency there.

Meanwhile, there is the related but separate problem of defining the

[8] I am grateful to Dr. D. H. Hill for information on his excavations there, and for generously supplying details of the coin find. For a recent summary, see P. Leman, 'Quentovic: état des recherches', *Revue du Nord* 72 (1990), 175-8.

character of the subsidiary, imitative series and of trying to determine its region of origin. It is stylistically homogenous and quite plentiful, and it imitates the York coinage of Series J: a far cry from Quentovic. This eclectic group, in so far as one can judge the sequence of its stylistic development, begins with 'mules' of Series G with Type 85 and Type 36, before settling down into straight copies of the Series G design, later simplified on reverse dies which are technically competent but with absolutely no aesthetic aspirations. Most specimens are unprovenanced, but the finds from Térouanne and Visemaretz itself belong to the eclectic group. Perhaps archaeological excavation will eventually show that both the main and the subsidiary series belong to Quentovic, as successive issues, although it is hard to see why there should have been muling part-way through the issue of an established type. One's instinct remains to see the eclectic group as the work of another mint. A find at Repton, and the York connection, together with the poor alloy, make one wonder about a fringe mint in the east midlands. Given that Series J reached the Low Countries in quantities, however, and probably was imitated there, it may be that the G/J muling is continental. There is no independent evidence for the date of the subsidiary group. In spite of its alloy, its origin is presumably contemporary with the issue of Type 36 or follows soon after.

There remain several specimens in miscellaneous styles, probably having no connection with either main group. Some, such as that from Corbie, and two from the Northampton excavations, with at least one from Domburg, and one catalogued below which inserts wolf's-head terminals into the design, are patently imitative. More than one has a doubly-outlined square on the reverse (Wymeswold and Bermondsey Abbey, which may well be from the same hand).

I

The simple character of the designs of Type 3a makes it difficult to establish a canon of official specimens. In doubtful cases, it will be better for the time being to err on the side of acceptance.

On the best early specimens, the hair is indicated by ten or a dozen straight lines, unpelletted, and brushed forward. Their general alignment is continued by a raft of similar lines below the diadem. The eye is a large almond-shape with central pellet. The mouth, which is a distinctive trait, consists of two faint dots joined together by a small C-shaped curve, making a moue. (This can be seen on the first two specimens catalogued below.) The boat-shaped drapery is made up of two or three freely-drawn curves. The cross in front of the face is elongated, but the position of the horizontal bar is variable.

The standard on the reverse contains a central annulet with pellet, four crosses pommee aligned X-wise, and four pellets between them. Often, one of the crosses is replaced by a group of three pellets. Two or more of the spacing pellets may be omitted (e.g. Garton-on-the-Wolds[9]). In the margins the ornament, when it can be seen, consists of a small cross pommee flanked on each side by two or three pellets.

A nucleus of specimens by the same hand, conforming to the above description, includes Garton 8 and a Hallum coin (Leeuwarden 270)

perhaps from the same obverse die,[10] Lockett 214a (catalogued below), and the Pyecombe (Sussex), Atherstone (Warwicks.) and north Essex finds.[11] The Arundel coin (also catalogued below) has quite different and more elaborate drapery, which is probably experimental. The characteristic moue is sufficient evidence, however, that it is part of the main series. Carlyon-Britton 153 appears to be another early coin of careful workmanship.

The Arundel and Lockett specimens contain 95 and 94 per cent silver respectively, the latter with 0.7 per cent tin.[12]

On Garton 7, Paris 12, and Wakering, one cross pommee is replaced by a group of three pellets, Garton 7 has only two spacing pellets, and

Wakering has none. The Whitby find[13] should probably be accepted as part of this little group because of the general similarity of its obverse to Lockett 214a. If the Wakering[14] find is also accepted, there is no obvious reason to reject Cimiez, le Gentilhomme 25 (which weighs 1.28g). Cimiez

[9] The two Garton specimens are illustrated in S. E. Rigold, 'The two primary series of sceattas', *BNJ* 30 (1960-1), 6-53.

[10] I was able to use Dr. D. H. Hill's photographs. Leeuwarden 270 = Dirks, pl. D, 20.

[11] For the north Essex coin, see D. M. Metcalf,

'Some finds of thrymsas and sceattas in England', *BNJ* 56 (1986), 1-15 and pl.1, 12.

[12] EPMA analyses by Dr. J. P. Northover.

[13] Illustrated in *BNJ* 1947 (1977), pl.1, 18.

[14] Illustrated in Rigold, loc.cit. (1960-1).

26 and 27 are certainly from the same obverse die as each other,[15] but from different reverses. Although they lack any hair below the diadem (as

does Cimiez 25), they too may be official.

When set against the canon, a good proportion of the finds from Domburg can be seen to be imitative. They manage to reproduce most or all of the formal features of the design, but can be faulted by the clumsiness of the nose, the eye, or the diadem, and by a lack of

compactness in the reverse. Paris 35, for example, has a retroussé nose, and a diadem shown by a row of pellets. Two of the three coins in the Hallum hoard (Leeuwarden 268-9 = Dirks, pl.D, 19 and 21) can be

dismissed as (early!) imitations. Both have a curved diadem consisting of a single line. Leeuwarden 269 has an inverted T and a row of pellets as additional design elements.

II

The subsidiary series, of poor silver, is easily recognized by the V-shaped ear and the triangular space in which the eye is enclosed. The corpus published in 1986[16] can be extended, but there are still so few specimens

[15] Again, with benefit of Dr. Hill's enlarged photographs.

[16] Biddle et al. (note 3 above).

of each variety that it would not be surprising if new varieties appeared. Those known are:

G2a. A 'mule' of G with Series J, Type 85, excavated as a grave-find at St.Wystan's, Repton. The stylistic irregularities of the bird-on-cross are

discussed in the original publication. (The obverse was originally interpreted as a copy of Series J, Type 36, of which two styles were included under the same rubric in *BMC*. The obverse of *BMC* 164, however, is better regarded as part of Type G2, and is listed as G2b here.) The Repton find weighs only 0.59g and is debased.

G2b. A 'mule' with Series J, Type 36. A distinctive hand holding the

cross is added to the design on *BMC* 164. There is a second specimen, from different dies, in Paris.[17]

G2c. The Visemaretz find of 1987 is from an extremely similar obverse die to *BMC* 164. On the reverse there are traces of what may be a double

square. If so, this variety is the prototype of the Wymeswold and Bermondsey Abbey finds, which are probably imitative. The die-similarity is such as to give strong grounds to assume that the Visemaretz coin is close in date to G2b.

A coin formerly in the F. Elmore Jones collection, 99,[18] with a cup-shaped hand holding the cross, borrowed from Series K, should probably be accepted as part of the subsidiary series.

A coin catalogued below has a similar hand. The style shows general deterioration, and the reverse margin has a row of five or six pellets, without a cross. The alloy contains 35 per cent silver, plus 5.8 per cent tin.

[17] Hill photos, no.3.
[18] *NCirc* 78 (1970), illus.99 (reproduced in enlargement in Biddle et al., loc.cit., Plate 1, no.8.

G2d. The outline of the standard is omitted on the reverse. The triangular ear and eye, and the two shallow curves of drapery, with pellet terminals, seem to be by the same die-cutter as the rest of the subsidiary series. The hand is omitted. The Térouanne find is of this variety.[19] A specimen below contains only 19 per cent silver, with 6.6 per cent tin.

III

Irregular and presumably unofficial imitations are relatively numerous in Series G. The two early copies in the Hallum hoard have already been mentioned. A coin from Domburg is of interest, as it shows how almost all the appropriate details, e.g. the moue of the lips, and the marginal crosses of the reverse, might be skilfully copied on a coin where the hair and diadem are, to our eyes, quite unconvincing. The diadem is curved,

with three large pellets at the nape, and the hair below it is brushed forward instead of being parallel with the hair on the crown of the head.[20] The find from Corbie may very well be by the same hand.

It is much more difficult to judge the Whitby and Aylesbury[21] finds, which appear to be by the same workman as each other. They may be official, but by another die-cutter.

Two other remarkably similar coins, of which one is from Wymeswold (catalogued below) and the other was in the Bird collection,[22] show that the die-cutting even of imitations can betray settled habits.

The two sceattas found in the excavations of St. Peter's, Northampton were both crude forgeries of Series G.[23]

[19] Metcalf, loc.cit. (note 6).
[20] Hill photos, no.25.
[21] Metcalf, loc.cit (note 11), pl.2, 31.
[22] Glendining, 20 November 1974, lot 10. 1.05g.

[23] J. H. Williams, *St. Peter's Street, Northampton. Excavations 1973-1976*, Northampton, 1979, at p.243.

DANISH SCEATTAS: SERIES X

THE SO-CALLED 'Wodan/monster' type, *BMC* Type 31, has the same facing head with long hair, beard, and moustaches seen on several sceatta types from eastern England, such as Series Z, and also (without the long hair) on Series H, from Hamwic. The significance of the design is uncertain, and a more neutral description such as 'facing head' might be better. Salin, in his general study of the Merovingian repertoire of motifs, calls it 'le masque humain'. Elsewhere he speaks of 'un masque divin, peut-être solaire'.[1] The other side of the coins of Series X, which is usually described as the reverse but which was often struck from the lower or obverse die, has the familiar monster with its head turned back to bite its own tail, with a long drooping crest, and with its foreleg tucked under its body. This is also a widespread motif, used for example on the sceattas of Series N. Salin calls it 'le monstre regardant en arrière', and equates it with the monster who guards a treasure.[2] Technically, then, the coins of Type 31 are probably mostly 'Monster/Wodans' rather than 'Wodan/monsters'. The conventional arrangement based on typology has, nevertheless, been retained in the text illustrations and on the plates.

The opportunities for a thorough numismatic analysis of Series X (in which Type 31 is the sole type) are excellent, because it survives in large numbers from more than one locality and because there are a dozen formal varieties. There is also a range of copies, many of them demonstrably struck elsewhere than in the main mint-place, which are full of interest. There were 173 well-preserved specimens of Series X in the Hallum hoard, and 120 (mostly less well preserved) among the Domburg site-finds. The Terwispel hoard contributes a further 161 examples, and there are numerous site-finds from Frisia and England (notably from Hamwic), and also from Ribe in Jutland, where the total of excavated specimens now exceeds a hundred.

Die-estimation shows that Series X was a very substantial coinage,

[1] E. Salin, *La civilisation mérovingienne*, vol.4, 1959, pp.221, 272, and 277.
[2] ibid., pp.220-1.

struck from at least 600 official reverse dies, plus a number of imitative dies.

Detailed analysis of the variation in style, etc., within the type is premature, however, until we have resolved the question where Series X was minted. An attribution to Frisia has sometimes been proposed. Although 120 seems a large number of site-finds from Domburg, and represents 12 per cent of the sceattas found there, at Ribe the type completely dominates the pattern of finds, with *c*.85 per cent. The proportion for Denmark is massively different from Dorestad (5 per cent) or from English sites (generally 2 or 3 per cent, but 9 per cent at Hamwic). One normally expects to find the greatest concentration of a type in its region of origin, and lower proportions further afield, where it comes into competition (as regards its share of the currency) with other, local types. On that basis, and in view of the very high proportional discrepancy between Jutland and any other region, there is a strong *prima-facie* case for an attribution to Denmark.[3] Ribe itself, where so many single finds of Series X have been excavated,[4] in archaeological contexts of craft industries at a sea-port, is the obvious candidate for the mint-town – rather than Hedeby, in the adjoining region of Schleswig, where extensive excavations have brought to light only a very few sceattas.[5]

The figure of *c*.85 per cent is, again, so very high as to imply either that the currency of Denmark was isolated, or that there was a policy of systematic reminting of incoming coinage. Given the trading connections with Frisia and the Rhine mouths, and the massive scale on which porcupines were minted, the Ribe finds strongly suggest a controlled currency.

A bare distribution pattern, unrelated to the geographical character of the regions involved – mere symbols on a small-scale map of north-western Europe – is hardly a sufficient argument if it is in question whether Series X was minted in Jutland or in northern Frisia. The percentages need to be set into a context of understanding of the relative prosperity and influence of the places that are being compared. Northern Frisia, where the Hallum and Terwispel hoards were discovered and where there have been other finds of Series X – from Bolsward, Ferwerd,

[3] D. M. Metcalf, 'A note on sceattas as a measure of international trade, and on the earliest Danish coinage' , in *Sceattas in England and on the Continent*, edited by D. M. Metcalf and D. H. Hill, Oxford, 1984, pp.159-64; id., 'Danmarks ældste mønter', *Nordisk Num. Unions Medlemsblad* 1985, 3-10.

[4] K. Bendixen, 'Sceattas and other coin finds', in *Ribe Excavations, 1970-1976*, vol.1, edited by M. Bencard, Esbjerg, 1981. The many finds from 1988 and 1990 await publication.

[5] See below.

276

and elsewhere in the province of Friesland – was a rural landscape liable to inundation, and dotted with terpen, or artificial settlement mounds.[6] Sceattas were in use, and were hoarded there, but it is implausible that they were minted there on a large scale.

The attribution of Series X to Jutland is nevertheless so unexpected that it demands critical scrutiny. Out of a reluctance, perhaps, to see the spell of the 'magic year' 800 broken in Scandinavian archaeology, an attempt was made in 1986 to discount the Ribe evidence by arguing that Series X is essentially of late secondary date, from a Frisian mint-place, and that it dominates the Ribe finds merely because the coin losses do not begin there until a relatively late date, when other common types of sceattas, in particular porcupines, had largely fallen out of use.[7] This argument is gravely compromised by the superb stratigraphy of the 1990 Ribe excavations (and by dendrochronological data from the site), where coins of Series X occur in quantity already in the 720s. It is further compromised by a specimen of Series X from a good dateable context at Hamwic (again with dendrochronological support). These prove, with no room for doubt, that the issue of Series X began early in the secondary phase. That being so, the attribution to Jutland rather than to Frisia or the Rhine mouths area, on the basis of comparative proportions of finds, appears to be incontrovertible.[8]

The Hallum hoard, which already contains almost all the known varieties of Type 31, is dated by Blackburn to c.715-20.[9] That would suggest a date of origin for the series no later than c.710. There seems to be a small discrepancy between the hoard chronology and the Ribe stratigraphy, and some adjustment downwards towards c.720 may be necessary in order to meet the dendrochronological evidence. There was a brief phase at Ribe (phase B2 and B3) when sceattas were being lost, including apparently secondary porcupines, before the heavy losses of Series X began.[10] The absence of X from the large Aston Rowant hoard,

---

[6] W. Op den Velde, W. J. de Boone, and A. Pol, 'A survey of sceatta finds from the Low Countries', in *Sceattas in England and on the Continent*, pp.117-45, at p.120.

[7] K. Jonsson and B. Malmer, 'Sceattas och den äldsta nordiska myntningen', *Nordisk Num. Unions Medlemsblad* 1986, 66-71. See also K. Bendixen, 'Skandinaviske sceattas-studier', ibid., 72-4.

[8] D. M. Metcalf, 'Nyt om sceattas af typen Wodan/monster', ibid., 1986, 110-20.

[9] M. Blackburn, 'A chronology for the sceattas', in *Sceattas in England and on the Continent*, pp.165-74, at p.170.

[10] I am much indebted to Mr. Stig Jensen and Mr. Claus Feveile, who allowed me to examine the finds from the 1990 excavations at Ribe and kindly explained the stratigraphy and interpretation of the site with me. Thanks are also owed to Mrs. Kirsten Bendixen and Mr. Jørgen Steen Jensen, for the opportunity to examine the coins from the 1988 excavations and to consider the implications of their stratigraphy. See L. B. Frandsen and S. Jensen, 'The dating of Ribe's earliest culture layers', *Journal of Danish Archaeology* 7 (1988), 228-34; S. Jensen, 'Dankirke–Ribe. Fra handelsgård til handelsplads', in *Fra Stamme til Stat i Danmark*, vol.2, pp.73-88.

concealed on Blackburn's chronology *c.*705-10, may provide a *terminus ante quem*, but because of isolation and distance, it should not be taken to prove absolutely that the first minting of Series X post-dates the hoard.

As well as being distinctive in its general style (e.g. the boldly dotted borders on obverse and reverse), Series X appears to have been very different in its underlying administrative arrangements from the later porcupines or the continental runic sceattas, with their undisciplined profusion of die-varieties. The bulk of the issue is regular in style, and is highly distinctive in its use of secret-marks.[11] These suggest that there was an elaborate system of control over the production of the coins. The evidence to support that claim arises out of the detailed classification of the type into a dozen or more formal varieties. The elements of the classification are set out below. The political and economic circumstances of such a large and coherent coinage would be hard to envisage in northern Frisia. Series X fits more persuasively into a context of royal power and initiative such as was capable, two or three decades after the issue began, of undertaking the first *Danevirke*.

The other seventh- and eighth-century coin finds from Jutland and its neighbouring regions offer some support to the hypothesis that Ribe was the mint-town for Series X. There are debased gold tremisses of the later seventh century from various localities including Dankirke, where 13 West European seventh- and eighth-century coins have been excavated, including 5 of Series X.[12] A stray find of Series X comes from Holmsland Klit, on the west coast of Jutland.

The generally early date of the Dankirke assemblage shows that coinage was reaching Jutland from the West (probably through Dorestad) for several decades before the minting of Series X began. Dankirke is quite close to Ribe and, to judge from the topography of the site, was at that time a rural manor which can have been of only relatively minor commercial importance, once the town had been laid out and developed. Ribe, with its fine harbourage, its trading connections, and its craft industries, was necessarily of political significance as one of the very few towns in the Northern Lands in the early eighth century. The dominance of Series X at Ribe, at a date when porcupines and other sceatta types had by no means fallen out of circulation in the Rhine mouths area or in England, thus implies that silver reaching the town was coined or recoined there. A hoard such as that from the coastal island of Föhr, consisting largely of porcupines, may reflect a sum of money on its

[11] Secret-marks are used elsewhere at this date only (and only probably) in Series H, Type 49.

[12] K. Bendixen, 'Finds of sceattas from Scandinavia', in *Sceattas in England and on the Continent*, pp.151-7.

way from the Rhine mouths area or Frisia towards Jutland, but which had not yet reached Ribe, to be recoined – or (as it contained a coin naming Milo) it may post-date the minting of Series X.

Five single finds of Series X respectively from Hedeby,[13] the south settlement at Hedeby,[14] and the Krinkberg[15] include no distinctive varieties, and thus offer no encouragement to suppose that there could have been a second mint for Series X at Hedeby, striking coins of the same basic design, – although if there had been a very minor or temporary mint there, the limited total of stray finds might well not be enough to reveal it.

I

Through a careful die-study based on the Hallum hoard, Barrett[16] has established the range of secret-marks shown in the diagram below. The symbols under the monster's head are systematically varied. They correlate convincingly with other details in such a way as to show that

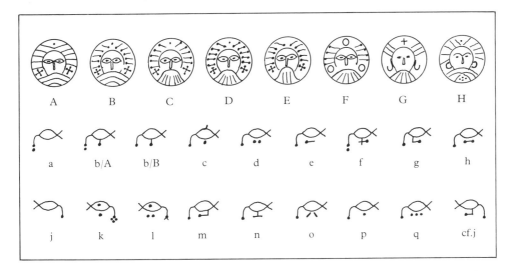

FIG. Barrett's scheme of classification of Series X, with additions (o, p, q, cf j, and D-H).

[13] Bendixen, loc.cit. (note 4 above) at p.66.

[14] G. Hatz, 'Münzfunde aus Haithabu, 1962', *Offa* 21/22 (1964/5), 74-9 and pl.8; id., 'Finds of English medieval coins in Schleswig-Holstein' , *Studies in Numismatic Method*, ed. C. N. L. Brooke et al., Cambridge, 1983, pp.205-24; H. Jahnkuhn, *Haithabu*, 8th edition, Neumünster, 1986, pp.85f.

[15] V. Hatz, 'Nachlese zum Krinkberg-Fund', *Hikuin* 11 (1985), 125-32 (and in *Offa* 10, 1952, 46-54).

[16] I am indebted to Dr. D. Barrett, who discussed his work with me and allowed me to see his provisional conclusions.

they represent separate blocks of the output of the coinage.[17] The correlative details are:

1. The use of one/two pellets at the end of the monster's drooping crest. Variety f regularly has two pellets, while most other varieties regularly have one.

2. A tuft sticking up from the monster's head is confined to variety c.

3. The facing head dies used with variety c mostly have 2 pellets above the head, instead of the usual one.

4. The facing head dies used with variety d often have crosses made up of a central pellet and two thin lines, in place of the usual cross pommee.

5. The scarce reverse ('facing head') varieties, B, C, and D are linked only with certain obverse (monster) varieties, in so far as the evidence is numerically sufficient to allow us to judge.

6. Variety b comprises two groups of coins, namely b/A, with two pellets on the crest, and b/B, with only one.

7. Varieties j, k, and l, on which the monster is laterally reversed, are scarce varieties, standing at some distance stylistically from the main body of material, as the treatment of the crest shows.

An obvious first step towards taking a critical view of the scheme derived from the Hallum hoard would be to compare the percentages of each variety in Hallum and among the Ribe and Domburg finds. If there were any clear discrepancy, the latter should probably be accepted as a more random sample. The hoard might, for example, have been concealed part-way through the issue of the series. In practice too many of the Domburg and Ribe finds are illegible or indistinct for the comparison to be better than approximate. They include singletons of two or three varieties not found in the hoard, and apparently of official quality, but in general the same range of varieties is represented, and varieties which are scarce in Hallum are also scarce at Domburg.[18] One could go through the list, noting for example that b/A and b/B are somewhat over-represented in the hoard, and so on, but the numbers are mostly too small and the margins of uncertain attribution too great for the exercise to have much statistical validity.

The diagram has been extended to include the few extra varieties represented in the Dutch collections, but absent from Hallum (o, p, q, cf.j, and D-H).

A similar comparison between the Hallum and Terwispel hoards is

[17] The evidence is derived from Dr. D. H. Hill's enlarged photographs of the Hallum hoard, without which its study would have been virtually impossible.

[18] The facing head versions C and D are more plentiful in the Dutch collections – arguably because they are English..

hampered by the damaged condition of most of the Terwispel coins. One can recognize most of the varieties among them, but estimates of the proportions of the different varieties are again subject to rather wide margins of error because of uncertainty.[19]

Estimation based on the Hallum material allows us to conclude that the main block of varieties (a to h) was struck from approximately 500 anvil (monster) dies, and approximately 600 upper (facing head) dies. As these estimates are derived from a single hoard, it is possible that they are to some degree under-estimates. There is, however, little sign of clustering or multiple die-duplicates. The over-all figures demonstrate a die-ratio in favour of the facing-head dies; but they conceal some variation.

Variety b/B (that is, the whole of version B), and also two other varieties on which there are regularly two pellets at the end of the monster's crest, namely b/A and f/A, have die-ratios of 2:1 or even higher. Most of the other varieties (where the figures are large enough to allow us to judge) are close to parity. In those varieties, either die could in principle be the obverse, but it is likely that the practice was the same as in variety b. One or two varieties deviate in the other direction. Of these c/A (or A/c?) is the most problematic. In the case of h/A, one should hesitate to accept a rather implausible numismatic conclusion on the basis of what may be merely a statistical quirk. (See, however, the comment on versions C and D, below.)

The evidence of the die-ratios, interpreted conservatively, suggests the hypothesis that there was a phase of rapid production, when more than one reverse die was used with each obverse die (and the simple secret-marking, or what was to develop into secret-marking, was on the obverse die), followed by a phase of more obviously varied secret-marking when the standard die-ratio was apparently 1:1.

As version B of the facing head design is more elaborate than version A, and accounted for only about a tenth of the total output of Series X, it is more plausible to place it at the beginning of the sequence that in the middle or at the end.

The main production of Series X may be provisionally tabulated, on the basis of the Hallum hoard, as follows:

---

[19] My figures, for what they are worth, were b/B, 6% (low), b/A, 23%, c, 24%, d, 9%, e, 11%, f, 8%, g, 6%, h, 10%, j, k, and l, 2%.

Variety	Specimens	Monster dies	Facing head dies	Survival coins/dies	Die-ratio rev./obv.
b/B	19	25	61	1: 3	2+ : 1
b/A	21	100	210	1:10	2 : 1
c/A	23	133	63	1: 5	1 : 2?
d/A	22	110	84	1: 5	1 : 1+
e/A	18	30	30	1: $1\frac{1}{2}$	1 : 1
f/A	13	15	78	1: 6	5 : 1
g/A	11	17	25	1: 2	1+ : 1
h/A	11	55	18	1: 5	1 : 3?
		485	570		

Thus far, the analysis of the varieties is reasonably clear. If one attempts to press it further, it becomes speculative. There are several more varieties, known only from one or two specimens, of which the style seems generally acceptable. When there is little with which to compare them, however, their status is difficult to determine. Version Q of the facing head, for example, is on record only as q/Q. It may be a brief issue from the Ribe mint – or, since the symbols to left and right of the facing head seem to be deliberately different- iated, just possibly from some other, minor mint under royal control in Jutland.

Were the secret-marks used in order to identify the coins struck by indiv- idual moneyers, some of whom were more active than others? Or were those varieties in which the estimated volume of production was smaller, such as e/A and g/A, in issue only for a short time? In other words, were the secret- marks in use concurrently or sequentially – or in a mixture of both? In the end, irrefutable evidence can only come from hoards concealed part-way through the issue of Series X. The survival-rate in the Hallum hoard (where, for example, variety b/A survives in 21 specimens from an estimated 210 facing- head dies) is erratic, perhaps for statistical reasons, and shows no clear trend. From this we should suspect that the wastage-rate from the currency was low.

A modicum of evidence may eventually be forthcoming from the Ribe excavations, where the specimens of Series X from the earliest stratified con- texts should in principle show us which are the early varieties. (In the later contexts, early and later varieties should both occur, since the former re- mained in circulation.) The evidential value of the earliest contexts depends on their being almost as early as the date at which Series X began.

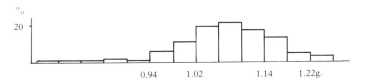

Fig. The weight pattern of Series X, varieties a-h (133 specimens, from the Hallum hoard).

The evidence of metrology is disappointingly uniform. The weight-standards of varieties a to h, and the degree of variation from the mean, appear to be all much the same. A histogram based on the Hallum coins[20] shows a normal, well-controlled coinage, with a modal weight of *c*.1.08g. If we break the evidence down, and look separately at b/B, b/A, and f/A; c/A and d/A; d/A alone; and e/A, g/A, and h/A, no interesting differences emerge. Perhaps d/A is a little more accurate than the other varieties.

Metal analyses by EPMA are available for nine specimens.[21] The silver contents are 96, 95, 92, 89, 87, 87, 84, 64, and 56 per cent, the last possibly an imitative coin. There is a rather poor inverse correlation with tin contents, which are mostly *c*.1.0-2.5 per cent, and almost certainly higher than would have resulted merely from recoining porcupines.

It is to be hoped that a major analytical project by EPMA based on the Hallum hoard will one day be undertaken. If variability of the alloy was tolerated, across a dozen or more formal varieties, a large number of analyses will be needed to reveal statistically valid differences. It would be naive, even then, to expect to find a single, progressive decline, offering a simple guide to chronology.

One suspects that facing-head dies on which the moustaches are more elaborate may be early, and that those on which the moustaches are represented, for example, by two shallow curves are late.

II

The mass of Series X consists of coins from the 600 or more dies, in a recognizably homogenous style, which make up varieties a-h. Outside that central block, there is a wide fringe of scarce varieties, known only in twos and threes,

[20] Again, I am indebted to Dr. Barrett for a list of the weights.

[21] Analyses by Dr. J. P. Northover of coins in the Ashmolean, Hamwic finds, and one specimen in the National Museum of Wales.

FIG. The characteristic style of Series X, recognizable throughout varieties a-h.

in a diversity of styles. The task of determining their status has to be undertaken piecemeal, variety by variety: there is no logic by which the results can be generalized. Many of the finds from Ribe will have been lost at dates after the concealment of the Hallum hoard, and a good proportion of them may have been minted after the concealment of the hoard. The absence of new formal varieties does not disprove that: it may be that in the later phase, the same formal varieties were continued, or the system of secret marking may have broken down into meaningless repetition (as happened, for example, with the later Northumbrian stycas). In any case, if Hallum is early, it is self-evident that either the minting of Series X was of brief duration in relation to the stratigraphy of Ribe, or there is a possibility of post-Hallum varieties. The post-Hallum phase is much less well understood, the coins having had a lower survival-rate and being often in poor condition. It is difficult to distinguish fully between late but official coins, and imitations. Some of the specimens are fairly obviously mere counterfeits, of poor alloy, out of which one cannot hope to build much of a pattern. Others are of careful and elaborate workmanship, and seem to be of good silver. A few of these are already represented in the Hallum or the Terwispel hoards. Several varieties, in looser and less accomplished styles, are known only from Low Countries and/or English finds. The label 'insular' has been used rather freely, but the question whether these were minted in Frisia, the Rhine mouths area, or England is a delicate one, and can be settled only on the basis of their relative frequency as finds, on a comparative basis. The statistics are, alas, inadequate to do more than suggest hypotheses here and there, because they are derived from such small numbers of coins. The most secure broad framework should be a comparison between Ribe, Domburg, and England, using the categories 'varieties a-h' and 'other'. Beyond the fringe of varieties that can be classed as direct copies of Type 31, there are other English types that use either the facing head or the monster as one of their designs. It is possible, but by no means necessarily the case, that they are copied from Type 31. If they are, there are chronological implications. But they may be drawing upon the general stock of motifs, that was shared by much of the Germanic world.

It is not possible, then, to give a systematic account of the remaining varieties of Series X. All that one can do is to list the more obvious styles, and draw attention to any coincidences of provenance.

The difficulty of the task is well illustrated by a pair of die-duplicates excavated at Åhus (Yngsjö), in southern Sweden, on a workshop site characterized by glass-making, metal-casting, antler-working, and the use of balances. The two sceattas were found in the upper part of an occupation layer, about 3m apart. It seems that they were separate losses. Their style is closely copied from the prototype, but they appear to be of virtually pure copper, and for that reason alone must be classed as imitations. Perhaps they were intended for use (what sort of use?) in a region where most people were still unfamiliar with a money economy. A third, separate find from Åhus is a clear specimen of variety g, of good alloy, and die-linked with a Ribe find.[22] It was found about 15m away from the other two sceattas.

These three coins, together with a porcupine from Helgö, and another from Fyn, are the only evidence so far recorded of the movement of sceattas eastwards from Jutland. The context of all or virtually all the copies will lie in the North Sea trade or in England.

FIG. Series X, variety j/A (Hallum hoard, = Dirks, pl.D, 28).

Lateral reversal of the monster is an obvious clue to imitation. Dirks pl.D, 28, for example, from the Hallum hoard, of variety j, has widely spaced pellets in the borders, and a much simplified treatment of the hair and moustaches.

FIG. Series X, variety n/A (Hallum hoard, Hill 164).

Variety n, which is known from two similar specimens in the Hallum hoard, is not guilty of lateral reversal, but its simple style is so much inferior to varieties a-h that one has little hesitation in dismissing it as unofficial.

Variety m is a mixed category. One of the two Hallum coins, will, again, command no confidence as an official issue.

One can add other nondescript coins, such as HPK 417, to build up a mixed

---

[22] Bendixen, loc.cit. (note 12 above).

Fig. Series X, variety m (Hallum hoard, Hill 394).

Fig. Series X, imitation (HPK).

bag of copies. The Fries Museum has one which seems to be the identical specimen from Reculver, published by Withy and Ryall in 1756.[23]

III

There is a substantial group of 'facing head' dies, which seem all to be from the same workshop, with a more naturalistic treatment of the beard and moustaches. They differ from the main series also in having hair with pellets at the outer end of each line (version C), or at both ends (version D), or at the inner end (version E: cf. B). It seems clear, from the recorded die-linkage, that in versions C, D, and E the facing head is on the obverse die.

Version C is usually, but not always, associated with reverse dies with a laterally reversed monster. The monster's crest is variable. Hallum 391, for

Fig. Series X, insular type, Variety C. Hallum 391 and HPK 426.

example, has a triangular group of three dots. BMC 147 and its die-duplicate HPK 426, ex De Man, are from the same obverse die as the Hallum coin, and so is a specimen in the Fries Museum, LFM 147. Hallum 300, HPK 403 ex De

[23] LFM 148.

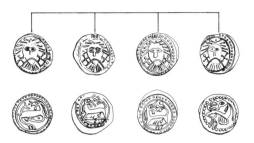

FIG. Series X, insular type, Variety C. Hallum 300; HPK 403; Six Hills; Lockett 243b.

Man, the Six Hills find, and Lockett 243b are four specimens which likewise share an obverse die. The Hallum, Leeuwarden, and Lockett coins have conceptually very similar reverses, laterally reversed, with the (pseudo-) secret mark attached to the neck rather than the oval of the head. On two of the three obverses one can see a rectangular panel with X, in the border at 12 o'clock: a detail that is seen again on a specimen found at Eynsham, Oxfordshire. HPK

FIG. Series X, Variety C. The Eynsham find.

FIG. Series X, insular type, Variety C. HPK 424.

424 has a group of 3 pellets above the facing head. There is another English find from Hindringham, Norfolk.

Version C has had a high survival-rate. Taken together with its absence or scarcity at Ribe, a region of origin other than Jutland is indicated.

Version D is perhaps an artificial category. It is known from one coin in the Terwispel hoard, but there is also a find from Rotherhithe (Stott 47), on which the hair is pelletted at both ends, which could be by the same hand as, for example, HPK 424, which is formally of version C. Both coins have a group of three pellets above the facing head.

Version E, on which the beard is shown by parallel lines, is known from the

FIG. Series X, Variety D. Terwispel hoard. The coin has been rubbed flat. The Rotherhithe find.

FIG. Series X. Variety E. Hallum 303 = Dirks, pl.D, 25.

Hallum hoard, 303 = Dirks, pl.D, 25. The monster has an elaborate crest, and its tail ends in a diamond marked out by four pellets.

One will suspect that Version C was itself subject to copying. Diagnostic details are the panel at 12 o'clock on the obverse, and the monster's gape on the reverse. Its jaws join the D-shaped outline of the head some distance apart, whereas on copies the lines of the jaws and head intersect in an X.

The crosslets on either side of the facing head are replaced by large annulets, with a third similar annulet above the head, in another little group of specimens with naturalistic beard (version F). A coin allegedly from the

FIG. Series X, Variety F. Cimiez hoard? Hamwic 123.

Cimiez hoard (Le Gentilhomme 73) and a Hamwic find (123) are from very similar obverse dies. A third specimen, now in the Fries Museum, is probably by the same hand. (It seems to have been acquired in England.[24]) On the second and third coins, the monster is laterally reversed. The Hamwic coin, which has an extra annulet on the reverse, below the monster's body, is severely debased, containing only 38 per cent 'silver' with 6.1 per cent tin and including 3.2 per cent lead. Its alloy presumably points to fraud rather than a late date. A similar find from Tilbury, struck badly off-centre, is catalogued below. It too has an extra annulet below the monster.

[24] Several specimens of different 'Wodan' types were bought: this one, LFM 1924.4.5.1, from 'C. C. Doming, Esq.'

FIG. Series X. Variety G. Lockett 243a.

Lockett 243a, with a pelletted lock of hair (?) to either side of the head, is more difficult to judge. It may be from the same source as versions C–F, but its style is not close enough for complete conviction (version G).

Still more doubt attaches to a grave-find from Wells cathedral, with large 'ears' to left and right of the head, and with a more original pattern for the beard and moustaches, enclosing a group of 4 pellets (version H).

FIG. Series X. Variety H. Wells.

Versions C–F find an echo in a few specimens with laterally reversed monsters, with distinctive large heads and beaks, but with obverses on which the beard and moustaches are not naturalistic. They copy the Danish prototype, with very shallow curves. Instead of the borders of bold pellets seen on the originals, and on versions C–G, these have grained borders, which serve to associate them as a group from the same workshop. They seem to be eclectic in having three annulets (as version F), or two annulets and a cross (Hamwic 122) or two crosses (Hamwic 121). A specimen at Leeuwarden was bought from Spinks in 1930.[25] These coins with grained borders are imitations of imitations, of the poorest alloy (20 and 26 per cent 'silver'). Their provenance does not exclude a continental origin.

FIG. Series X. Imitations of the insular variety, with grained border. Hamwic 121 and 122.

What of the region of origin of versions C–F? Can we, indeed, assume that they share a common origin, when some of them are so debased? If we make that assumption, on the grounds that the style of all the versions could refer

[25] 1930-5-6-10. It weighs only 0.73g.

289

them all to the same die-cutter, then there is a strong case for concluding that they are English. The list of definite English provenances is extensive. We have: C, Costessy, Six Hills, Hindringham, Eynsham Abbey; D, Rother-hithe; F, Hamwic, Tilbury; and perhaps H, Wells. *BMC* 147 (version C) is a pre-1838 accession and very probably an English find. These nine finds make up almost a quarter of all English finds of Series X. That is a far higher propor-tion than at Domburg or in Denmark. If versions C-F had been continental, there would be no reason for them to reach England in greater proportions, in relation to the rest of Series X, than in their region of origin – unless they were selectively exported, because of their poor alloy, as an exercise in fraud.

Within England, the distribution of versions C-F apparently differs from that for the rest of Series X. The Danish coins show an intriguing concent-ration in Middle Anglia, and it is tempting to search for some special explan-ation. It will be prudent, howver, to reserve judgement. Versions C-F, in comparison, seem to be more peripheral, but it is difficult to find any unified explanation. Two finds from Norfolk and one from Leicestershire are likely to be diagnostic, because they reflect the highest regional concentration. They suggest a possible parallel with Series BZ, which also includes very de-based specimens. The finds from Tilbury and Rotherhithe could have been carried by east-coast shipping. The Hamwic provenance (123) is difficult to relate to those from Norfolk, unless the variety's origin were continental. The grave-find from Wells could have entered Wessex via Hamwic. Hamwic itself may well be a special case: the high proportion of Series X there (compared with east Kent, in particular – which was nearer to the continental sources for Series X) hints at a Jutish trading connection.

The occurrence of versions C-D in the Hallum and Terwispel hoards is intriguing, if they are English. Again, it hints that traders may sometimes have selectively sent distinctive sceattas back to the place they came from, or where it was thought that they would be acceptable. Hallum is also valuable because it demonstrates an early date for the beginning of the imitative series. The Hallum hoard includes other sceattas from the eastern coastlands of En-gland, from very early in the secondary phase.

An English attribution should be regarded as provisional until clearer evidence is available. Chemical analyses of the Hallum imitative specimens would be of interest. The awkward choice, meanwhile, seems to be between an origin in the east midlands, and selective export from Frisia of debased coins for the English market.

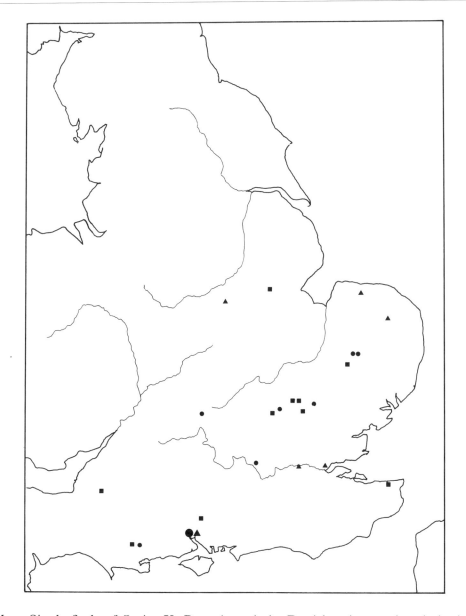

MAP. Single finds of Series X. Round symbols: Danish coins or close imitations. Triangles: insular copies of Varieties C-F. Square symbols: other styles, including those with W-shaped beard; and also unverified specimens. (30 finds, including 9 from Hamwic.)

IV

Another stylistic group of imitations is characterized by a forked or W-shaped beard. The Royston finds 42 and 43 exemplify the style, which is more delicate and composed of smaller pellets. The crosses on each side of the facing head are made up of disconnected pellets. The recorded finds are English – a third comes from West Stow, and there is another which, in so far as one can judge from a dark photograph, might be related, from Hanford, Dorset.[26] As the style seems to be unrecorded at Domburg, the coins are in all probability English in origin. The monster, which can face left or right, is strongly in-

Fig. Series X. Insular variety with W-shaped beard. Royston 42, 43.

fluenced by Series N. The suggestion has been made that this variety is the prototype for the Danish issue. It would be imprudent, however, to base any chronological conclusions on the link, which could just as plausibly have been in the other direction. The W-shaped beard can be traced back as far as c. 710, in the Kings Lynn imitation of Type 66.

A similar W-shaped beard is seen in Type 30, which has been interpreted in another section as an echo or continuation of the earlier Series BZ. Type 30 is found in two styles, of which the finer style, Type 30a (*BMC* 135), has pelletted borders that are almost certainly copied from Series X.[27]

Another version of the facing head, without the characteristic lens-shaped eye-sockets, is paired with an elaborate annulets-saltire reverse. Hamwic 124

Fig. Facing head with W-shaped beard. Hamwic 124.

is a specimen of excellent alloy (91 per cent 'silver', with only 0.1 per cent tin). Another specimen, from the Norwich area, is in the Stewartby collection.

[26] *Proc. Dorset NHAS* 101 (1979), 138.

[27] There is a problem with a coin in the Fries Museum which appears to be absolutely identical with *BMC* 145. Miss Archibald has kindly verified *BMC* 145 for me, and is entirely satisfied of its authenticity. Perhaps the coin in Leeuwarden was acquired as an electrotype?

Again, an English origin is probable.

Stripping out the imitations helps to make clear how stylistically compact the main block of Series X was. The duration of its issue is something about which evidence is hard to find. All the common varieties are already present in the Hallum hoard. They may well have remained in circulation for many years after their issue dwindled or ceased. Callmer has reviewed such clues as are to be found to the chronology of Series X, and has explored the purposes of eighth-century minting, and developed the idea of regionally shifting coin stocks.[28] In the last resort, however, only a comparative study of the age-structure of a sufficient number of hoards can provide secure evidence.

[28] J. Callmer, *Sceatta Problems in the Light of the Finds from Åhus* (Scripta Minora, Kungl. Veten-skapssamfundet i Lund, 1983-4, no.2), Lund 1984.

PLATE 9

CONTINENTAL SCEATTAS

SERIES D

The coins of Type 2c have been arranged tentatively, placing those with correct runes first. A small run of specimens from Aston Rowant illustrates the two weight-standards seen in the hoard. A coin which is apparently very base, and a plated coin (from the Birchington grave-find) are placed last. Recognizing copies is otherwise difficult; many coins in poor style are probably official.

TYPE 2C: HEAVY SPECIMENS

158 1.28g. ↑↙ 95% 'silver'. Seriffed 'initial cross'. Evans bequest, 1941.

159 1.24g. ↑← Bt. from finder, 1992. Found Bawsey, Nf.

160 1.26g. 95% 'silver'. Bt. from finder, 1986. Found St. Nicholas-at-Wade, K.

161 1.11g. ↑↓ 95% 'silver' (XRF, O.199). Bt. 1974, ex G. E. L. Carter colln.

162 1.14g (worn). ↑← Blundered runes. Evans bequest, 1941.

163 1.23g. ↑↓ 94% 'silver' (cf. XRF, 91%, O.197). Bt. 1974, ex G. E. L. Carter colln.

164 1.13g. ↑↑ 94% 'silver'. Given by A. H. Baldwin and Sons, 1986, ex Sotheby, February 1984.

165 1.10g. ↑↑ 95% 'silver'. Pseudo-runes, resembling **M**. Seriffed 'initial cross'. Evans bequest, ex Birchington grave-find. C. Roach Smith, *Coll.Antiq.*, vol.1, pl.23, 4.

166 1.21g. ↑↘ 92% 'silver'. Bt. Sotheby, 17 July 1986, lot 184, ex Aston Rowant hoard.

167 1.16g. ↑→ 86% 'silver'. Pseudo-runes, resembling **M**. (Cf. 165.) Bt. Sotheby, 17 July 1986, lot 184, ex Aston Rowant hoard.

168 1.20g. ↑↖ 86% 'silver'. Bt. Sotheby, 17 July 1986, lot 184, ex Aston Rowant hoard.

169 1.23g. ↑↑ 96% 'silver'. Obv.die in degenerate style. Bt. Sotheby, 17 July 1986, lot 184.

170 1.16g. ↑↘ 96% 'silver'. Simple pseudo-runes. Bt.1987. Found in Norwich area.

TYPE 2c: LIGHT SPECIMENS

171 0.99g. ↑↘ 96% 'silver'. Simple pseudo-runes. Bt. Sotheby, 17 July 1986, lot 184, ex Aston Rowant hoard.

172 0.89g. ↑↓ 90% 'silver'. Bt. Sotheby, 17 July 1986, lot 184, ex Aston Rowant hoard.

173 0.95g. ↑← 69% 'silver'. From the same obv. die as 172. Rev 'legend' has **O** at 9 o'clock. Bt. Sotheby, 17 July 1986, lot 184, ex Aston Rowant hoard.

174 0.84g. ↑← 81% 'silver'. Pseudo runes and **A** laterally reversed. Simplified reverse. Bt. Sotheby, 17 July 1986, lot 184, ex Aston Rowant hoard.

PLATE 9

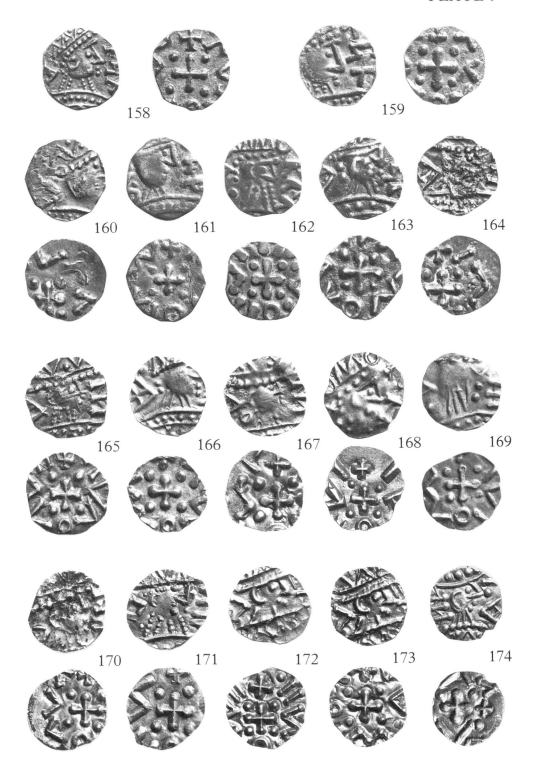

158

159

160　161　162　163　164

165　166　167　168　169

170　171　172　173　174

PLATE 10

175 0.88g. ↑↑ 94% 'silver'. Given by J. Eric Engstrom, 1986. Found Thetford, Nf.

176 0.92g. ↑← 95% 'silver'. Head left. Bt. 1987. Found in East Anglia?

177 0.88g. ↑← 93% 'silver' (XRF, O.196). Two large runes. Bt. 1974, ex G. E. L. Carter colln.

178 0.67g. ↑↙ 93% 'silver' (XRF, O.200). Bt. 1974, ex G. E. L. Carter colln.

179 0.54g. ↑↑ Obv. die in degenerate style. Bt. from finder, 1991. Found Bawsey, Nf.

180 0.90g. ↑↓ Bt. 1974, ex G. E. L. Carter colln.

IMITATIONS OF TYPE 2c

181 1.05g. Very debased. Obv. laterally reversed throughout. Bt. from finder, 1991. Found Bawsey, Nf.

182 0.55g. ↑← Plated on base-metal core. A/D 'mule'. Evans bequest, 1941, ex Birchington grave-find. C. Roach Smith, *Coll.Antiq.*, vol.1, pl.23, 5.

TYPE 8

183 1.32g. ↑↑ as illustrated. 94% 'silver'. Bt. British Museum, 1937, ex. T. G. Barnett bequest duplicates.

184 1.18g. ↑↓ as illustrated. 95% 'silver'. Bt. Sotheby, 17 July 1986, lot 191, ex Aston Rowant hoard.

185 1.21g. ↑↗ as illustrated. 87% 'silver'. Bt. Sotheby, 17 July 1986, lot 191, ex Aston Rowant hoard.

186 0.62g. ↑↓ as illustrated. Plated on base metal core. Surface, 85% 'silver'. Bt. Sotheby, 17 July 1986, lot 191, ex Aston Rowant hoard.

'MULES' OF SERIES D

187 1.12g. ↑← as illustrated. 95% 'silver' (cf. XRF, 94%, O.198.) Square ⊏ in reverse 'legend'. The third rune on the obv. is apparently *p*. Type 2c/8 'mule'. Bt. 1974, ex G. E. L. Carter colln.

188 0.75g. ↑↙ Series E/D double-reverse 'mule', copying the **VICO** variety. Bt. from finder, 1991. Found Bawsey, Nf.

189 0.65g. ↑↓ Series E/D double-reverse 'mule', copying the 'plumed bird' variety. Bt. from finder, 1991. Found Bawsey, Nf.

PLATE 10

175   176   177   178   179

180   181   182

183   184   185   186

187   188   189

PLATE 11

SERIES E: THE FOUR EARLY VARIETIES

THE 'PLUMED BIRD' VARIE-TIES (J, K, AND L)

190   0.97g. ↑← 93% 'silver'. Variety J. Cross pommee beneath bird's neck. Quills set closely. Groups of 3 pellets on reverse set closely. Ashmolean Museum, old colln.

191   1.15g. ↑→ Variety J. Two pellets beneath bird's neck. Bt. from finder, 1992. Found Bawsey, Nf.

192   0.95g. ↑↑ 96% 'silver'. Variety J. Cross pommee beneath bird's neck. Evans bequest, 1941.

193   1.33g. ↑↘ 96% 'silver'. Variety J. Cross pommee beneath bird's neck. Bt. 1974, ex G. E. L. Carter colln.

THE VICO VARIETY

194   1.15g. ↑↑ 95% 'silver'. Sub-variety 2 var., with groups of 3 pellets on rev. (experimental?). Evans bequest, 1941, ex Rolfe. Found Barham, K.

195   1.24g. ↑↑ 95% 'silver'. Sub-variety 2. Christ Church (Barton, 1765).

196   1.33g. ↑↙ 96% 'silver'. Sub-variety 3. Bt. 1987.

197   1.10g. ↑↗ Sub-variety 1. Bt. from finder, 1992. Found Bawsey, Nf.

198   1.24g. ↑← 94% 'silver'. Sub-variety 1b. Bt. British Museum, 1937, ex T. G. Barnett bequest duplicates.

IMITATION OF THE VICO VARIETY

199   1.31g. ↑← 72% 'silver'. Bt. Sotheby, 17 July 1986, lot 190, ex Aston Rowant hoard.

VARIETY G

(The coins are arranged in accordance with Blackburn and Bonser, in *BNJ* 1987, pp.99-103.)

200   1.23g. ↑↑ 93% 'silver'. Variety G0 (groups of 3 pellets on rev.). B. and B.8 (this coin). Magdalen College.

201   1.24g. ↑← 96% 'silver'. Variety G1. B. and B.13 (this coin) as G2. Bt. 1988. Found near Cambridge (Wilbraham?)

202   1.18g. ↑↗ 95% 'silver'. Variety G2. Bt. 1987. Found near Norwich.

203   1.21g. ↑← Variety G3, with legend AZO. Ashmolean Museum, old colln.

204   1.24g. ↑↙ 95% 'silver'. Variety G3. B. and B.22 (this coin). Evans bequest, 1941.

205   1.06g. ↑↙ 94% 'silver'. Variety G4. Bt. 1988, ex finder. Found Oxborough, Nf.

PLATE 11

190   191   192   193

194   195   196   197   198

199   200

201   202   203   204   205

PLATE 12

IMITATIONS OF VARIETY G

206   1.18g. ↑↑ 94% 'silver'. Bt. 1987 (English find).

207   0.90g. ↑↑ 94% 'silver'. Bt. Christies, 4 Nov.1986, lot 358. Found Caistor-by-Norwich, Nf.

208   1.12g. ↑→ Bt.1990 (English find).

VARIETY D

209   1.16g. ↑→ 94% 'silver'. Bt. Sotheby, 17 July 1986, lot 186, ex Aston Rowant hoard.

210   1.20g. ↑↘ 88% 'silver'. Bt. Sotheby, 17 July 1986, lot 186, ex Aston Rowant hoard.

211   1.29g. ↑↑ 96% 'silver'. Bt. Sotheby, 17 July 1986, lot 186, ex Aston Rowant hoard.

IMITATION OF VARIETY D

212   0.72g. ↑↑ Bt. from finder, 1991. Found Bawsey Nf.

'MULE' OF SERIES E, VICO VARIETY

213   1.19g. ↑↓ 95% 'silver'. Obv. imitates Type R1 (*epa*). Bt. from finder, 1987. Found Woolstone, Brk.

SERIES E; KLOSTER BARTHE VARIETIES

The coins are arranged in no very good order, mainly on the basis of their silver contents, style, and provenance. Die axes are as illustrated.

214   1.35g. ↑↙ 94% 'silver'. Bt. Baldwins, 1986, ex H. A. Parsons, 103.

215   1.14g. ↑↗ 91% 'silver'. Same dies as 214 (diff. die-axis). Anonymous gift (before *c*.1960). Found Binsey, O.

216   1.08g. ↑→ 95% 'silver'. Bt. Baldwins, 1986, ex R. C. Lockett 215.

217   0.91g. ↑↖ 84-87% 'silver' (XRF). Bt. F. W. Kuhlicke, 1966, who had bought it many years previously from an old lady in Bedford. See 235-6 below.

218   0.86g. ↑↘ *c*.84% 'silver'. Bt. 1974, ex G. E. L. Carter colln.

219   1.26g. ↑↖ 92% 'silver'. Bt. Baldwins, 1986, ex R. C. Lockett 215.

220   1.28g. ↑↖ 80-82% 'silver' (XRF). Ashmolean Museum, old colln.

221   1.16g. ↑↙ Bt. 1974, ex G. E. L. Carter colln.

222   1.09g. ↑→ 89% 'silver' (XRF). Thomas Knight bequest, 1795.

PLATE 12

206   207   208   209   210

211   212   213   214   215

216   217   218   219   220

221   222

PLATE 13

223 1.22g. ↑↖ 70% 'silver'. Uncertain provenance (ticketed 1966).

224 1.20g. ↑↙ 95% 'silver'. Bt. D. M. M., November 1988, ex finder. Found West Wycombe, Brk.

225 1.28g. ↑↖ 93% 'silver'. Bt. 1974, ex G. E. L. Carter colln.

226 1.36g. ↑→ 69% 'silver'. Bt. 1974 ex G. E. L. Carter, ex Lockett 218b.

227 0.91g. ↑↘ The nick is modern. Uncertain provenance.

228 0.77g. ↑↗ Evans bequest, 1941. If old ticket is correctly associated, found 'near Abingdon(?)' (description, 'queer beast 3 legs, square with T T / \' agrees).

229 0.81g. ↑↙ Bt. from finder, 1991. Certainly from north Lincolnshire, and reportedly near Keelby.

230 1.17g. ↑↓ 88% 'silver'. Bt. Baldwins, 1987.

231 1.32g. ↑↓ 92% 'silver'. Bt. Baldwins, 1987.

232 0.98g. ↑↖ Bt. from finder, 1992. Found Bawsey, Nf.

233 1.19g. ↑↑ Old colln.

234 1.19g. ↑↖ 85% 'silver'. Bt. Glendinings, 21 May 1940, lot 17 (part). Ticketed 'Compton find', and believed to be from the Staffordshire Compton. See no.96.

235 0.89g. ↑← Same provenance as no.217.

236 0.91g. ↑↖ Same provenance as no.217.

237 1.12g. ↑↖ 86-88% 'silver' (XRF). Bt. Baldwins 1966, ex 'Franceschi' parcel. *ANSMN* 1969, no.8.

238 1.24g. ↑↗ 83% 'silver'. Same provenance as no.237. *ANSMN* 1969, no.9.

239 1.10g. ↑↑ 78% 'silver'. Same provenance as no.237. *ANSMN* 1969, no.12.

Cf. Lockett 216d.

PLATE 13

223   224   225   226   227

228   229   230   231   232

233   234   235   236   237

238   239

PLATE 14

240   1.31g. ↑↗ 81% 'silver'. Same provenance as no.237. *ANSMN* 1969, no.14.

241   1.10g. ↑↑ 67% 'silver'. Same provenance as no.237. *ANSMN* 1969, no.17.

242   1.30g. ↑← 88% 'silver'. Bt. D. M. M., 1988, ex 'Franceschi' parcel, *ANSMN* 1969, no.18.

243   1.28g. ↑↖ 88% 'silver'. Same provenance as no.242. *ANSMN* 1969, no.26.

244   1.35g. ↑↑ *c.*80% 'silver' (XRF). Same provenance as no.242. *ANSMN* 1969, no.28.

245   1.22g. ↑↙ 84% 'silver'. Same provenance as no.237. *ANSMN* 1969, no.33.

246   1.26g. ↑← 73% 'silver'. Bt. 1974, ex G. E. L. Carter colln., ex Lockett 218a.

247   1.04g. ↑↖ 64% 'silver'. Bt. 1987, ex finder. Found between Beverley and Woodmansey, Y.

248   1.04g. ↑↙ H. de S. Shortt bequest, 1975, ex Miss P. J. Gordon, Wyke Regis (? South Hampshire find).

249   0.55g (broken). ↑↑ Same provenance as no.248.

250   0.74g. ↑↖ 77% 'silver'. Bt. Baldwins 1986, ex H. A. Parsons 103.

251   1.08g. ↑↑ 46% 'silver'. Same provenance as no.242.

252   1.11g. ↑↑ 30% 'silver'. Bt. D. M. M., 1988, ex finder. Found Remenham, Brk.

253   0.69g. ↑↓ Bt. from finder, 1992. Found Bawsey, Nf.

254   0.39g. ↑↙ Base. Given by J. Booth, 1978.

PLATE 14

240 241 242 243

244 245 246 247 248

249 250 251 252 253

254

PLATE 15

SERIES E: FRANEKER VARIETIES

255 1.08g. ↑↑ 82% 'silver'. Bt. 1987. Cf. Dirks, pl.B, 15.

256 1.37g. ↑↑ 90% 'silver'. Bt. Baldwins, 1986, ex H. A. Parsons, 103. It is not certain which phase this specimen belongs to: its weight is high.

257 0.98g. ↑↓ 42% 'silver'. Bt. 1987.

SERIES E, TYPE 53

258 1.10g. ↑↗ 96% 'silver' (XRF). Bt. Grantley sale ii, 27 Jan.1944, lot 712 (part).

259 1.29g. ↑→ 94% 'silver'. Bt. Baldwins, 1986, ex J. W. Stephanik colln., F. Muller, 12 Dec.1904.

260 1.10g. ↑↑ 94% 'silver'. Bt. Christies, 4 Nov. 1986, lot 365. Found Caistor-by-Norwich.

261 1.17g. ↑↖ 94% 'silver'. Bt. 1987. Found in the Thetford area.

262 1.03g. ↑↓ 94% 'silver'. Bt. from finder, 1986. From the line of the Fosse Way near Six Hills, Le. SK 648241.

SERIES E, TYPE 4 VAR.

263 1.20g. ↑↙ as illustrated. 91% 'silver'. Ex Bodleian Library, old colln.

SERIES E, TYPE 12/5

264 1.09g. ↑↓ 25% 'silver'. Bt. Baldwins, 1987, ex A. F. Baldwin colln.

THE 'MAASTRICHT' TYPE

265 0.81g. ↑ ↖ c.45% 'silver'. Evans bequest, 1941.

266 1.17g. ↑↘ 74% 'silver'. (Imitation?) Given by D. M. M., 1 November 1988, ex finder. Found Woodeaton, O. *Sceattas in England and on the Continent*, p.202 and pl.10, 22.

SERIES G

267 1.10g. ↑↓ 95% 'silver'. Given by D. M. M., 1 November 1988. Found near Arundel, Sx.

268 1.06g. ↑↑ 94% 'silver'. Bt. D. M. M., 1989, ex C. Hirsch colln., ex Lockett 214.

PLATE 15

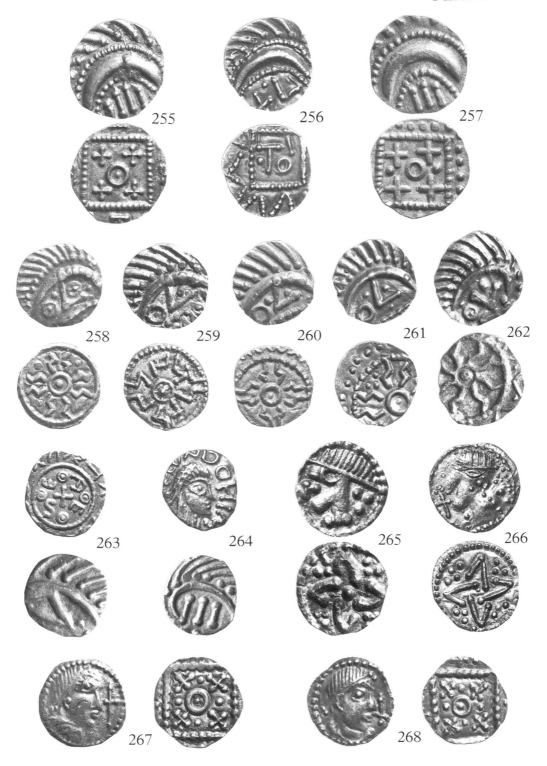

255

256

257

258

259

260

261

262

263

264

265

266

267

268

PLATE 16

269 0.89g. (flaked). ↑↖ Bt. from finder, 1991. Found south of Atherstone, Wa.
270 1.06g. ↑↗ c.85% 'silver' (XRF). Bt. L.

IMITATIVE SERIES

271 0.94g. ↑↓ 35% 'silver'. Bt. 1974, ex G. E. L. Carter colln.
272 1.10g. ↑↖ 19% 'silver'. Bt. 1974 ex G. E. L. Carter colln.

Pennycord, resident of Selsey (finder?), 1950. Found on Selsey beach.

OTHER IMITATIONS

273 0.98g. ↑↑ 45% 'silver'. Animal-headed truncation. Ex Bodleian Library, old colln.
274 1.13g. ↑ ↖ 37% 'silver'. Bt. from finder, 1986. Found near Wymeswold, Le.

SERIES X

Barrett's varieties are sketched in the text, above.

275 0.97g. ↑↗ 87% 'silver'. Monster with tuft. Barrett var.c. Evans bequest, 1941.
276 0.82g (chipped). ↑← 96% 'silver' (enriched?). Defective 'monster' die, but probably an official coin rather than an imitation. Barrett var.d. Ex Bodleian Library, old colln.
277 0.61g (weathered). ↑↓ 88% 'silver'. Barrett var.f. Bt. 1974, ex G. E. L. Carter colln.
278 0.83g (weathered). ↑↓ 56% 'silver'. Barrett var.g. Bt.1936, from E. V. Evetts, ex W. Evetts (Tackley) colln. Found within parish of Tackley, O.
279 0.85g. ↑↓ 84% 'silver'. Elaborate beard and

moustaches. Barrett var.n? Evans bequest, 1941.
280 1.03g. ↑↘ 63% 'silver'. One pellet at end of crest. Barrett var. b or p? Bt. 1987. Found in the Thetford area.
281 1.32g (encrusted). ↑↓ 95% 'silver' (surface enrichment?). Barrett var. illegible. Evans bequest, 1941.

IMITATION

282 1.05g. ↑→ Obverse var.F. Bt. from finder, 1989. Found Tilbury, Ess.

PLATE 16

269 270 271 272 273 274 275 276 277 278 279 280 281 282